GROWING UP IN CHRIST

It's Relationship, Not Religion

VOLUME I

MEL SPEARS

©Copyright 2026

IBG Publications, Inc.

Published by I.B.G. Publications, Inc., a Power to Wealth Company

Web address: www.ibgpublications.com

admin@ibgpublications.com / 904-419-9810

Copyright, 2026 by Mellai Spears

IBG Publications, Inc., Jacksonville, FL

ISBN: 978-1-971850-00-9

Spears, Mellai
Growing Up In Christ Volume I-It's Relationship, Not Religion

---

All rights reserved. This book, or its parts may not be reproduced in any form, stored in a retrieval system, or transmitted in any form, by any means-electronic, mechanical, photocopy, recording or otherwise, without prior written permission of the publisher or author, except as provided by the United States of America Copyright law.

Printed in the United States of America.

DEDICATION

To my greatest gifts from God, my greatest inspirations to live, and my best presentation of love: my Star; my Sun and my Moon. You three are my Sky. There are no words to describe how instrumental each of you have been in this continued journey of me 'Growing Up in Christ.'

Each of you consistently provides me with intricate details on how to be just a little better in this world we share. There is not a day that I am not learning from the three of you. Because of that, I am stronger and wiser as well as grateful. You three have taught me the meaning of true love, especially you, "my stars" being the oldest, you have been on most of this journey with me. You have ridden with me through each rough sea, always encouraging me to continue to push forward, never jumping ship.

I appreciate and admire your respect for me and how you honor me as your mom even with all my flaws. You have given me courage to believe in myself simply because you believe in me. You see me as your hero and because of that you too are mine.

I feel so blessed to be your mom; you are blossoming into such an amazing young woman of God. I am so grateful to God for all my trial and tribulations, and it is my hope that you will see through my faith in Him that anything is possible.

Thank you for being a beaming light in my darkest moments and for being mommy's "armor bear" in all my times of need. You are my Stinky-Butt, no matter how old you get you will always be my baby! I love you more, and more and more and more and more!

My Moon and my sun, you both have stretched mommy beyond a capacity that only the strength of God could have gotten me through. Thank you both for challenging me for the better and for loving me beyond even your comprehension currently. My Sun, you are already a powerful young lady in the Lord, and I am so thankful for your steadfastness and already strong belief in God's powerful word.

My Moon, you, my child are my only begotten son. For that, I am blessed. I love you both.

Forever, Mom

THANK YOU

I'd like to take a moment to thank everyone that made this project possible.

The Bible says in **Romans 8:28**, *"For we know that all things work together for the good of those who love the Lord in which are called according to his purpose."* Therefore, nothing is wasted.

There is a blessing or a lesson in every experience in our lives. That means there is great value in every situation and person we encounter. When we think of life from that perspective, we can grow from our experiences. In return, we can allow others to grow as well.

We have a wonderful manual to help us in life. Unfortunately, it's a never-ending journey so neither we nor them may not always get it right. Thankfully, we are given grace, and we can give others grace. Only then can we walk in genuine love and forgiveness.

Because of this grace I have been given, I am grateful for those who have stretched me beyond my own capacity. Those who, because of how they may have or have not treated me, forced me to turn to our Lord in prayer. I have grown so much from each encounter, and I now know each experience was part of the making of 'me.' So, thank you all for being an intricate part of my 'growing up in Christ.'

Whether good or bad, you helped birth this project and those to come. I love you all with the love of Christ, and each of you know who you are.

May God bless each of you in your respectful place and meet your every need.

SPECIAL THANKS

To those of you that were there for me over the past six years as this project developed, to the moment my manuscript was submitted, I have nothing but pure gratitude in my heart for you. Whether it was financial support, physical support or spiritual encouragement, I am forever indebted to you. Without you and the love in you from God, this may not have been possible.

Thank you for the long hours of keeping my baby boy occupied. Thank you for being an ear to listen to me as well as a shoulder to cry on. You have been my rock, an anchor to keep me on track and a blanket of security in those moments when I was feeling like I could not do it. You are my blessing from the Lord, and I will never ever forget you or all you have done.

May God replenish all that you poured out to me during this journey. I love you with the REAL kind of love!

FOREWORD
-James Spears-

For over ten years, I have had the unique privilege of witnessing a remarkable transformation; one that can only be described as the work of God. What I have seen is the journey of a woman who once did not necessarily believe in Christ, to one who now not only believes in Jesus, but places Him and His Word above everything in her life.

What makes this even more meaningful is that I did not always know her as my wife. There was a time when I knew Mel simply as a friend. Yet even then, I could see that something was taking place in her life, something real, something powerful that could not be ignored. Over time, that friendship grew, and today, I am honored to call her my wife.

This book reflects that transformation.

Mel Spears is not writing from theory she is writing from experience. Her life tells the story of what it truly means to grow in Christ. From a place of unbelief to belief, and now to a life fully surrendered and centered on Him, her journey is both authentic and inspiring.

For those who are strong in their faith, this book will serve as a powerful example of iron sharpening iron. For those who believe in Christ but have not yet fully committed to living a Christ-centered life, it offers a clear and compelling invitation to go deeper. And for those who may not yet believe, this book has the potential to open hearts and change lives just as her life itself is a testimony of what God can do.

There is something within these pages for everyone. No matter your background or where you are on your journey, you will find pieces of yourself here. The depth of what she has overcome and the honesty with which she shares makes this book both relatable and transformative.

Let me tell you about this woman.

She is a devoted mother who gives her all to her children. She is intelligent, driven, and committed to continuous growth, both personally and academically. She is compassionate and selfless, leading and serving through her nonprofit work with a heart for others. But above all these things, her greatest attribute is her love for Christ. She lives her life grounded in the Word of God, seeking Him in all that she does.

From her childhood, through her teenage years, and into adulthood, her story will capture your attention and hold it. You will not simply read this book you will experience it.

It is an honor for me to introduce this work to you not only as someone who has witnessed her journey, but as the man who now walks beside her in it.

Whether you are just being introduced to Christ, or you are continuing to grow in your relationship with Him, this book will meet you where you are.

So, take your time, reflect, and allow yourself to be inspired as you turn the pages of one of the most powerful examples of what it truly means to grow in Christ.

With love and much gratitude,

James Spears

FOREWORD
-Pastor C. Smith-

It is both an honor and a joy to write this foreword for Mel Spears a woman whose life and walk with Christ I have had the privilege of witnessing firsthand.

Since 2023, what began as a simple acquaintance has grown into a deeply rooted and meaningful friendship. Over time, we came to recognize that our connection was not by chance, but by divine alignment. We are, in every sense, soul sisters united not only by shared experiences, but by a mutual hunger for God and a desire to grow in Him.

From the moment we connected, there has been a consistent and undeniable growth in Mel's life. I have watched her evolve spiritually in ways that are both powerful and inspiring. There were times when others would refer to her as a "babe in Christ," but I found myself compelled to lovingly challenge that label. The authority with which she speaks, the depth of her understanding, and the anointing that rests on her life all testify to something far greater than spiritual infancy.

Mel's journey reflects what it truly means to grow in Christ not through religion, but through relationship. Her walk is not defined by routine or ritual, but by a genuine, intimate connection with God. It is evident in her words, her actions, and the way she carries the presence of the Lord.

This book is not just a collection of thoughts or teachings; it is an extension of Mel's lived experience her growth, her surrender, and her unwavering commitment to becoming who God has called her to be. As you read, I encourage you to open your heart and allow the same Spirit that has shaped her journey to speak into your own.

Mel Spears is a living testimony that when one pursues God wholeheartedly, transformation is inevitable. Her life reminds us that true spiritual maturity is not measured by time, but by depth of relationship.

It has truly been a pleasure knowing her, growing alongside her, and witnessing the hand of God upon her life.

With love and honor,

Pastor C. Smith

TABLE OF CONTENTS

Chapter 1

AND THE JOURNEY BEGINS...

Becoming a believer in Christ was not on my list of things to do. To be honest, I had never dreamed that I would be a believer due to what I had witnessed in my limited exposure to what I knew of the body of Christ.

Growing up, there were several "believers" among me. They believed in God but as I understand today, they denied the powers within as they were not necessarily living what they claimed to believe. I'd say much like the Pharisees in the Old Testament who would teach the Bible but would not live what they taught. Jesus referred to them as hypocrites and warned the disciples to follow their words, but not their actions.

Well, at that time, this was confusion for me as I had not yet had a relationship with Christ, so I did not understand what to follow. There was just no clear way to know. Those limited, yet very impressionable encounters as a young child caused me to struggle greatly, trying to differentiate between the believer and the non-believers.

In many instances, they all seemed to blend right in together. What I saw then is the same thing I see playing out today as well. I am hearing it is a very similar experience for others as well. Those who believe and those who do not believe are in many ways difficult to differentiate between the two. I believe if we look at the lifestyles and consider the characteristics of those who claim to be believers in Christ and non-believers, you could very easily assume they were the same.

Both Believers and non-believers today are out doing each other in the actions of being 'of the world' and not just in it. God, however, is not confused by our actions and knows the difference. He was very clear as the word says we should be set apart, conforming not to it. Therefore, there should very well be an easy distinction between the two, a believer and a non-believer.

Those who believe/follow Christ, are often mimicking the same lifestyle and characteristics as those that do not follow Christ. This led me to have many questions as a child; like many children, questioning is what I did.

I have never been a shy person and very vocal concerning my thoughts. What my mouth didn't say, my face most certainly did. I remember being as young as around ten years old asking all kinds of questions I really needed answers to. I genuinely wanted to understand the whole 'God thing.'

The questions I asked, those who said they were believers, would answer in a way that would only confuse me more. This led my little mind to ponder and only assume even further. I'd wonder if they were hiding something, they didn't know the answer, or they simply didn't appreciate me asking. I was very curious, and I was simply seeking understanding.

At the time my little mind would stop at nothing to get answers to my questions. I was thirsty, yet I unknowingly was looking in the wrong place to quench my thirst. That is until I was taken to a pastor who very firmly told me to stop asking questions. The pastor warned me that my questioning God was a sin, and God didn't like it. Being the child I was, I respectfully told the pastor that I was not questioning God, I was questioning people of God and they themselves were not God. I didn't know a lot, but I knew that much.

The pastor was not pleased with me nor with my sincere response. In fact, he was quite offended and chose to no longer entertain my curiosity or in his mind maybe, my disrespectful questions. He then sent me on my way. This puzzled me even further, pushing me further away from God.

This is the issue most have today, we go to people and put our trust there instead of in our God. Unfortunately, God gets the blame for it. Imagine that God gets blamed for what people choose to do, go figure.

Thankfully, His word says, "He will never leave us nor forsake us." Regrettably, we leave Him.

Yet like the prodigal son, He is always waiting for our return. Of course, I had no idea at the time and the questions in my little heart and my sincere desire to know went on for several more years before I simply stopped asking. I didn't stop because I had the answers or clarity to my thoughts, I stopped because my desire to know shifted my little belief into not believing at all. The people of God were not helping, instead they were hurting me.

At that time, what I should have done was turned to the source Himself, but how could I have known this? I had no guidance, everyone "of God" I turned to, pushed me away. I had concluded; it all had to be just a big old lie that people had told repeatedly to put fear in everyone's heart. I mean, what else would explain the lack of explanation from so many?

I felt like Dorothy from the Wizard of Oz, after she had become lost. She was simply looking for directions and answers, just someone, anyone to direct her back home. Like me, the further Dorothy looked, the more distant from home she felt she was and the less she became aware of her surroundings or the people she thought she knew.

It was as if I was on this yellow brick road like Dorothy. It seemed so promising, even scary at times, but promising. All I wanted was directions to get back 'home.'

I met many people along the "yellow brick road" of my spiritual

journey. What I learned was that many of those I encountered seemed spiritually strong, brave, entertaining and some were so full of the word. What I soon came to realize is, like me, they too were searching for something. They were not as brave, strong, or as full of the word as they portrayed themselves as being, it was a mirage. I understand now, they too, like Dorothy and I, were searching and trying to find their way home as well. They too had become lost along the way.

Unfortunately for me, like Dorothy and her crew, when I finally made it to where I thought I'd get the answers, it didn't happen. I felt this whole story of "God" was like the man behind the curtain once Dorothy made it to Emerald City. He was just a loud voice with no power and no answers to His own questions.

It wasn't until Dorothy stopped believing or trusting in people that she realized what she needed was already inside of her. It was time to find **me**, dig within and find my own answers. Had I listened to that little still voice inside of me instead of those voices from my childhood, I would have known that statement couldn't have been any truer.

As **Jeremiah 1:5** says, *"God knew me before He formed me in my mother's womb."* Although I could not remember at that time, I had already been in a relationship with God and the home I was seeking was indeed within me. I just needed my spirit to be restored and for my heart to be cleaned as the word says.

Again, I had no idea at that time. When I turned 19, I was already a 'go against the grain' type of child and it became even more difficult to convince me about any topic, especially the "wizard" behind the curtain. I was a 'prove it' type person, only believing if I saw it with my own eyes. Unknowingly, I was running from God, and the enemy was having a field day or years with me, so to speak.

Of course, life began to happen, and God allowed it. This forced me into a completely different environment than I had ever imagined. I became linked with a group of individuals considered "Knowers" if you will. Like me, they needed to know the ends and outs of a thing before believing it. This was perfect for me, or so I thought at the time.

How could it **not** be? They were so knowledgeable and answered all the questions I had about "God." I was truly with my kind of people, and we were going to prove to the world the God **they** thought they knew was not the 'actual' God.

The more I fellowshipped with them, the "wiser" I became. I became so wise in my "walk," I chopped down anyone in my path that wanted to sell me on any of the "Jesus" story outside of Him simply being a prophet or a regular person just like me. I mean at least now I began to believe in some sort of 'God' again, right? I just did not believe the way I had been raised to believe in HIM.

As I think back now, I don't really recall being raised on the Jesus I have come to know. I knew 'Jesus' as, if you sin, you go straight to hell. Which is true in a sense but unfortunately, it does not depict the love of Jesus or the beauty of having a relationship with our Savior. In fact, it negates His entire purpose of being, as well as His self-less sacrifice.

Becoming a "Knower" gave me a sense of hope, a sense of belonging. What I had been taught and had come to believe about Jesus was that He was simply a man like anyone else, no one special. He was born of a regular woman who was impregnated by a regular man, so nothing miraculous there, right?

The whole 'Jesus' story that many had become to believe was a sense of manipulation from the "slave master" and just an evil method of control. I was taught as we focused on color, that everyone in the Bible were of African descent. The white man, "the devil" had changed the names, the description, and the narrative of the people just as they had the ancestors of "people of color." You get the picture, and the sort of logic that is unfortunately still being taught and believed today by man. It creates such confusion as well as division.

Many want Christ to identify with them, and whatever their race is, instead of us identifying with *Him* and running *His* race. I am not saying there is no truth to some of this theory, what I am saying is that should not be the focus. As those are actions of man, not God. His *race*, we all have access to, has nothing to do with the color of our skin, our origin, our status etc.

In fact, **Galatians 3:28** states *"There is neither Jew nor Greek, there is neither slave nor free, there is not male and nor female, for you are all one in Christ Jesus."* This means anyone who desires to have access can, no matter who we are or where we come from.

Christ came on the scene in physical form as He had always been with us since the beginning. He is the word; He is the living word. I will go further into that in G.U.I.C Volume ll, if the Lord says the same.

The word also says in **John 3:16**, *"WHOSOEVER" believe, shall not perish but have everlasting life."* So, we simply must be a "WHOSOEVER," this is where our maturity begins. It has nothing to do with anything but our souls. We simply need to accept and believe Christ as our Savior allowing Him to lead us through the rest.

Lord knows, I wish I had known this back then. I could have helped save some souls, starting with my own. Instead, for years I continued this path of destruction hungering for more wisdom, yet I was still spiritually dead. As much as I thought I knew, understood, and sincerely believed and had studied; even if proven to be true, there was still something missing.

I became thirstier for something; I just didn't know what. Now I know that I was searching for the truth, however with the lack of a physical Shepherd and being spiritually dumb to the 'Shepherd' Christ Jesus. This led me to feel alone. I felt empty, but to others I would come off as if I was sound in what I had learned to believe. I sincerely wanted to help them to believe and get away from the "lie." However, deep down inside, I knew there was still something I was missing. I kept feeling a nudge from what I now know was the Holy Spirit.

As time went on, I began to seek things in the physical that I lacked from my childhood to help me when I was feeling alone. I thought marriage would be the missing link to the joy I was lacking, the fill to the emptiness inside. It just had to be the answer, especially since I was a product of a broken home. Marriage had to be what would fill this ever-growing void within me.

Nope, that only deepened the thirst. After multiple trials and tribulations, I married then divorced. I was still lost and became angry and quite frustrated with my life. What do I do, where do I find answers? I have read, spoken to others, tried to fit in everywhere

I went. No matter what I did, I still felt as if there was a pull on my life.

I simply could not shake this feeling.

I turned back to God, yup the one that I was convinced so many times, was not real; at least not in the since the world would believe. No longer was I looking to people to fill this void, I knew God Himself needed to fix this. I could just feel this was bigger than me. Therefore, I went into prayer.

I would ask God, "If there is something you want from me, show me." He never showed.

I understand now, God does not move when *we* want Him to but in His own timing. Nor does He move how we *think* He should move. He's God, not a genie in a bottle. You could not have told me that then of course. Like the rebellious wretch I was, I continued the path of destruction.

My only goal was to continue to debunk anything from the Bible and to push the doctrine that I was so knowledgeable about at the time. Besides, I asked God to show me Him and He never responded.

Spiraling out of control in yet another lost marriage and reunited with the previous, I now have two children with him. Because this was what I thought would fill that still pressing void in my life, I returned to what I already knew was ***not*** the issue; the issue was me. I was thirsty, yet still nothing, not marriage, children nor money was quenching it.

I became angry.

This relationship fails again, so now I swear off relationships. Including relationship with any kind of God; besides, it's all a lie. "Keep all of it and the false hope that comes with it," so I thought to myself! But oh Boy, I can almost see God laughing at me as He had something in store for me that I was not quite ready for.

Can I be honest and say that there are still some days I feel like I am not yet ready for what He has I store for me and the assignment on my life? Have you ever felt like that in this walk? Like it's simply too much and you just want to throw in the towel. My God, it is a struggle at times, but only when we try to carry it ***ourselves***.

Take the journey with me as I uncover my personal process of "Growing Up in Christ" or what I consider the "University of Christ." The true meaning of Higher Education in my opinion. The one place you do not get a degree of any sort and graduation isn't until we are called home to be with the Lord. It's a place of study where you may have to be held back a time or two, not just based on your works or lack thereof, but also based on the God given assignment on our lives for that purpose.

I believe my own view interrupted my peace because I was allowed to conform in many aspects to the ways of my world. This was due to my disobedience and the lack of understanding of the importance of a relationship with Christ Jesus. I should have been adhering to the voice of the Lord and following the instructions of **His** way instead of my own. His way was simple in developing my purpose to be a testimony and example to the world of true Kingdom. My way was just causing me to be an example of religion.

What I was not aware of then is there was already and still is a plan for my life. This plan was specifically organized with me in mind and created well before I was even a thought to my parents. A plan perfectly structured by our Heavenly Father. A plan so magnificent, not even my parents themselves could have come up with on their own.

Thanks for the grace of God, because the plan is one that I could not sabotage if I simply believed. **John 3:16** states *"...whomsoever believe, shall not perish, but have everlasting life."* That and the mere love of God would guide me to put off the old man and walk in the newness of the Lord.

Unfortunately, like many who say we believe before, I got caught into the web of growing up in the religion of church, instead of 'in relationship with Christ.' As I grew in His plan, I have learned that His ways are not my ways and that His thoughts are not my thoughts; but ultimately His plan will work for my good.

Romans 8:28 states it like this: *For I know all things work together for the good of those who love the Lord and who are called by His name.*

I was not at that time aware of this scripture from the Bible, however it was indeed playing out in my life as it had and is now planted in my heart. It is one of my many rock scriptures that I tap into frequently when I feel as if I cannot go any further in this walk. I confess that even THIS will work for my good if I simply believe.

What is a rock scripture for you? Take moment to pause to write down one of the scriptures that helps you get through until God brings you to, in the space below.

Self-Reflection

I have left a blank page after each chapter throughout this book to allow you to take a moment and reflect on your own life.

- ✓ What areas do you see you may need to continue to grow in?
- ✓ Can you relate in any way to any of that of what I have encountered?

You can also simply take notes to re-visit later. The goal for this is to help us all look at our own journey. Mine may not look like yours or yours look like your loved ones or friends, however we all have our own path to salvation. I'd love to hear yours. More details will be given further in the book.

____

____

____

____

____

Chapter 2

YAHWEH, NOT MY WAY ...

Things are beginning to look up for me in several amazing ways. I'm doing well in this financial company, no worries there. I'm putting all my efforts and focus only on what concerned my children, my health, and my work. Nothing else was of any of my concern.

I was purposely beating the sunup, and it was beating me down daily. Money was flowing, and I was making wonderful strides to get back on my feet after the divorce. I looked amazing and felt even better. I was in a great place; nothing could stop me.

However, just as I became comfortable in where I was with work, kids, health etc., the feeling of a void set in. Something was still missing and whatever it was, it would not release me.

I shopped until I dropped.

"What is this that is missing in my life?" I thought, "Why can't I seem to find joy?" I was happy, so I thought; but there was no peace. I pondered, "It must be me. God, what am I missing Father?"

This time, I was now open to hearing what I may not have heard before as I secretly still wanted answers to the never-dying questions from my childhood. Deep down, I knew God was the only one who could fulfill this thirst, but I didn't know how.

What I did know, I needed to do something different. I mean I've been across the country and back, first college graduate in my family, lived in luxury places, traveled, married, and divorced. I had kids and was doing well in my career and was even at my best fitness level ever. But there was still something missing.

Ok Lord, "I'm ready," I told myself.

I was open and willing to give this God a true chance because everything else I had tried failed and left me even more empty than the last time.

So, I did it. I put on my big girl panties, and I dove in headfirst. If I was going to do this, I needed to give it my all, right?

Well, on one accord, I'm still not believing in this false man-made son of His that the slave masters had so cleverly come up with to control the slaves. Nope, not doing it or all bets were off. I let Him know I wanted to hear from Him.

I did Bible studies, and my God things were looking promising. I was sold out to God, my savior, not Jesus but the Father. He saved my soul. Glory be to God.

Don't get me wrong, I had even then, a great respect for Jesus, He was a great man. He performed wonderful works like the others in the world, 'in my mind,' but He was *not* my savior. I even believed He was a great prophet but not like that of the stories told. He in my mind was a mere man, he bled as I bled, how dare I bow down to that? Oh boy, did I have some growing up to do in Christ.

Well, it is getting better.

I found myself really becoming closer to God, going to church during the week as well as doing weekly bible study. I did not quite understand it but did what I could. I am a new creature, and at this point I still don't know any scriptures except a couple learned from childhood. But I was in the word faithfully, my life was changing, and no longer did I have the same desires I had previously had. I am simply amazed at this point and giving God all the praise.

I was listening to gospel, fellowshipping with others and even went to church on a weekday. I even had sisters in the word and a cousin helping me to better understand the King James version of the Bible. Oh, I was so into what God had for me and things were going great.

Everything was great until one night when I patiently waited for the arrival of my little girl. I was expecting my ex-husband (the children's father) to bring her home by a particular time, only He didn't.

I became enraged.

I did not understand because this man knew my schedule. I

didn't keep late hours, and I wanted my child home at a particular time. This was not anything new with my ex and part of the reason we divorced; he lacked the ability for me to rely on him in any manner. Especially concerning keeping a schedule. I could not understand why this night it hit so much harder for me.

Whelp, God did because He had other plans for me that night. Plans I was not quite ready for, but He showed me that I had no choice at that point. I believe God was tired of my mess-ups.

I cried out to Him for answers.

"What is happening God? I am serving you diligently, I am seeking after you like a hungry child, and You allowed this?"

I was mad, angry and then I did the unthinkable. I said, "God, tell me what you want from me, or leave me the HELL alone."

Yup, I had been serving God in my mind well and there was no reason He should not help me with whatever I wanted or needed Him to do. It was His word that said He'd give us the desires of our hearts. I felt like He was not keeping His word, or at least in my mind He wasn't.

I went to bed that night, with no regret. I felt vindicated in how I felt and acted towards God; how dare He not answer me? What I didn't understand at that time, is God works on *His* time not mine. I had been serving God but denying His son. What I wasn't aware of is, that no matter how much you seek God, if you deny His Son, you deny Him, it's Biblical.

John 14:6-11 says, "Jesus saith unto him, I am the way, the truth, and the life: no man cometh unto the Father, but by me."

I thought God was a genie in a bottle and answered my commands, twisting up His words to fit my narrative and He needed to move when I asked Him to. That was not who or what our God is, there is a requirement that is necessary to get the access that I was seeking.

Unfortunately, that requirement was Jesus Christ, though He had already died for me washed away my sins, I simply needed to accept Him as my Lord and Savior to access the benefits of the Kingdom. I had not yet become a Kingdom Citizen, but low and behold the Bible says, every knee shall bow, and every tongue shall confess the name of Jesus. Some of us are just a bit more stubborn than others.

To God be the glory, nothing gets wasted in God. That same stubbornness I had in the world doing it my way, God will soon use in the Kingdom equipping me to do it **His** way.

Can I tell you the word did not lie, this walk is not for the swift nor for the strong, but for them who endure to the end. Lord have mercy on me as this was only the beginning of the end of my wants and needs being exchanged for the completion of His will for my life.

Have you too had an experience where you had a wrestling among your members? What have you learned from your experience? Use the space below as well as the empty page provided if needed, to elaborate on that experience?

____

____

____

____

____

MEL SPEARS

Chapter 3

ASK AND YOU SHALL RECEIVE

I woke up the next morning ready to start my day as normal. I felt no regret for the night before when I demanded God to speak.

I went about my day as normal, even saying my prayers and not thinking twice if I needed to apologize to God for what I said. I worked, hung out with friends, and even worshipped, but who did I think I was? I was ignorant, proud, and lacked a relationship with Christ, otherwise I would not have been so disrespectful. However, in my carnal mind, I was doing a great thing. I mean I still greeted Him in the morning; I prayed right? It must have meant something because I had had a very nice day, right?

It was time for me to begin preparing for another realtor's course the next day. I remember watching Sarah Jakes late in the evening, as I did my hair. Again, giving no further thought to the demand I had put on Heaven the night before.

As normal, I searched for an online service, and I unknowingly stopped at a testimony on YouTube of Sarah Jakes who was sharing a message of how she was a young mom. I was truly touched by her story. Even in awe of how God turned her life around.

She spoke about Jesus but that just went in one ear and out of the other. Because remember, in my mind, Jesus was great but not what had been described in the Bible; or so I thought. Isn't it amazing how we can pick and choose from the word what we want to believe? We do this with hope of conforming what *we* want or do not want from it instead of us conforming to what it wants from us?

I was so lost.

Even now after proclaiming to "Love" God, I was still doing things my way and denying His son. As I think back on it now, I feel so blessed and humbled that God still sees fit to use me to even write this book. *Again*, nothing is wasted in God's Kingdom.

Let's continue with the story. The more Sarah Jakes spoke about Jesus, the less I listened, I walked into the bathroom to finish my hair. As I put another flex rod in, Sarah's voice became faint. I then recall a moment when I heard a voice. I wasn't hearing with my ears it was more of a spiritual voice, something I never heard before. The voice spoke with a question and an answer followed.

"You want to know what I want from you? What I want from you is for you to go into ministry."

I froze and slowly I looked around in panic. I was the only one here, it was only me in the bathroom. So, who is speaking to me? My flesh asked because it couldn't process the voice, but in my spirit it was familiar. Immediately, I KNEW who it was. I had never heard the voice before, but it was clear that the Holy Spirit was present.

I began weeping uncontrollably; I was filled with tremendous guilt. I was overwhelmed, grateful, scared, and sorry all in one moment. I felt the love, but I just didn't understand. I felt lighter, but I didn't understand. After years of me slaying people concerning Christ Jesus, He still thought enough of me to not only show up and talk to me, but He desired to use me in God's ministry. Now I understand what I didn't understand at that time is what 'being used' entailed. What I knew immediately is that God thought enough of me that even with all my mess, disobedience, and rejection of His son, He had already equipped me for the assignment.

I cried harder.

I was condemning myself, dwelling and looking over my life: the lies, the deceit, being divorced and all my other sins. How is it possible I can do anything in God's kingdom? People will judge me; they will say I'm not enough. The enemy was again winning, and I had no idea.

I had already repented and accepted Jesus as my savior, and was still thinking, "Heck the Holy Spirit thought enough of me to visit me personally, yet I was allowing the enemy to keep me stuck in what I had already been forgiven for." Falling even further into condemnation.

After crying and praying, with puffy eyes, swollen cheeks, and a runny nose, I shakenly began to call those I had been connected to as I grew closer to God. He knew I needed to be encouraged because at the time, I didn't have enough faith yet to encourage myself.

It was well after midnight at this point. Hair rollers half in and half out, I never turned off the TV, but it was silent. I could only hear the negativity from the enemy, and I was having a pity party.

Everyone I called, no one answered, so I began texting them. I remember as I texted huge tears falling from my face; I was so sorry for how I treated God. Then a call came in, the voice said "HALLELUJAH, I already knew God was going to use you mightily in the Kingdom, PRAISE the Lord and fear not, you are in good hands. God loves you and Jesus died for your sins, so you are now made new; embrace it sister!"

She continued to say, "The day I met you, I was drawn to you, and I saw the anointing on your life. You didn't believe in Jesus, but He believed so much in you."

I cried harder.

I asked how was it that He forgave me, she answered, "This was all part of God's plan. He knew this day would come."

Jeremiah 1:5 says, *"For I know the plans I have for you,"* declares the LORD, *plans to prosper you and not to harm you, plans to give you hope and a future."*

She continued encouraging me, "So, understand that there is nothing you have done that Jesus hasn't forgiven you for."

What I didn't know at that time was what had all already been written and had begun to take place right before my eyes.

Colossians 2:13 says, *"And you, being dead in your sins and the uncircumcision of your flesh, hath he quickened together with him, having forgiven you all trespasses."*

This all took place some years ago, yet it still feels so fresh as He truly saved my soul that day from the pit of hell. Each time I think about it or tell my testimony, I can still feel the very moment when I was set free and the shackles had fallen off my feet. Of course, at that time, I still did not quite understand why. But the word is true, it says we would be given peace that would surpass all understanding.

What I have learned and now understand is that the enemy was only doing his job. There was no way he wanted to lose another one of his followers to the Kingdom, and of course in my ignorance, he thought he had me.

We must know that once we repent with a sincere heart for anything we have done, except for Blasphemy against the Holy Spirit, we are forgiven. So, the guilt I was feeling about God was just me still stuck in my stinking thinking. God had forgiven me; I simply needed to forgive myself allowing God through Jesus to continue developing me.

Then I received a call from another sister. She shared with me a similar thought that she knew it was only a matter of time before I would surrender to Christ. By the time she called, I was a little calmer than before as it was going into daylight. I literally had no more tears from crying and repenting all night.

She shared with me a story about a man in the Bible; a man I had never heard of. Saul, who like me, had slayed anyone that would follow Christ Jesus. I was blown away by what I was hearing. Unlike Saul, I was verbally killing them; he however was physically killing them. Nevertheless, we both were in sin towards Christ, in a sense. We like many others were doing the work of the enemy and swore we were doing the work of God.

Have you ever found yourself in that place of being tricked by the enemy, thinking you were doing the work for God but instead were stuck in religion doing the work of the enemy? How did you overcome it? Could you possibly still be stuck in religion and lacking a relationship?

Take a moment to reflect on that.

She continued sharing that Saul had his encounter with Christ, while on his way to Damascus to confront more Christians. There was a bright light from Heaven, followed by a voice. The voice questioned Saul and took away his eyesight for three days, allowing him to see spiritually instead. This encounter like mine, made then Saul a new man.

Saul too immediately knew who he had encountered. Just as I was convicted, Saul no longer had it in his heart to crucify Christ's followers. I now had the heart to become a member of the body of Christ, like then Saul, now Paul, to encourage others to do so. As you read further into Saul's story, you will see his name was changed from Saul to Paul. I like to explain to those who get confused that the S (Stuck in Sin) represents a time before his encounter with Christ if you would and P (Paid the Price) after Christ.

From that day on, the same passion I had to slay Christ's followers is the same passion God has given me to share the good news of salvation. Isn't it amazing how God will repurpose what the enemy tries to use for evil and to our demise? God cleans it up, washes us with the blood to be used for good in His Kingdom; so again nothing is wasted.

Genesis 50:20 says, *"You intended to harm me, but God intended it for good to accomplish what is now being done, the saving of many lives."*

Joseph was speaking to his brothers who had some years before, been used by the enemy to kill him. This was out of jealousy and was the trick of the enemy, but glory be to God, there was already a plan on Joseph's life that not even Satan could stop.

After hearing what a sister in the body had shared with me about Paul, formerly Saul, I felt a wonderful lift in my spirit. I felt even lighter now, no longer in condemnation as I was now seeking after the spirit and no longer the flesh. I had accepted and received the love of Christ; I now had my access.

I was slowly beginning to truly get a better understanding of what Jesus was all about. The word says He did not come to condemn the world but to save the world. So, unlike what I had understood or had believed before. He is indeed the Savior, my Savior. But boy, that was only the tip of a huge iceberg coming. Little did I know, yes to Christ meant saying no to the devil, and he was not going down without a fight. This made me an even greater target.

What I know now that I didn't know then is Satan is a sore loser and does not fight fair. He Is a liar, and his only objective is to kill, steal, and destroy. But in all essence, Satan cannot do anything that God does not allow.

Though we are forgiven, there are still consequences for our actions. But God's grace will keep us as we go through. That is what happened to David in **2 Samuel**. God just wants us to learn and grow from our actions not repeat them again.

Taken our power from the enemy. I like to put it like this, Satan is in a sense an employee of God's, he can only do what God allows, nothing more, nothing less. But it is our job to focus on God and do our part to keep the enemy in the unemployment line, remembering his benefits are already denied.

Self-Reflection

What was your coming to Jesus' moment? Was it like mine, something like the Saul to Paul experience, or something totally different?

I would love for you to share. Use the space below as well as the empty page provided if needed, to elaborate on that experience.

____

____

____

____

____

____

____

____

____

Chapter 4

RUTHLESS

During the time of my Christ discovery process, I had been reconnected with a man who I had never met in person. We had been virtual business partners for a short time. He owned a school and seemed to be very comfortable. He was kind, tall, dark, and handsome from what I saw in his pictures, but we never stepped outside of business mode.

When he resurfaced and learned of my new walk with Christ, he reminded me that he told me early on that I missed my calling and would be a great counselor someday. What he shared further on is what he was saying was I was being called into the Kingdom of God. He said that he didn't want to scare me as he knew I had not fully believed in God, much less Christ. Like others had already stated to me, he knew this day would soon come when Christ would recruit me.

As we spoke further, he shared his feelings and interest in getting to know me and how he had been looking for me for some time. As I looked back, I realized he had been interested in me but covered it with business. He said he had been divorced for six years and had not dated due to work. He expressed that the moment he saw my picture; he knew I was his wife. He continued to share he was a Bishop and that God sent him to save me and take care of me. He began referencing the Bible, the book of Ruth to be exact.

Now here I am a single mom at this point, fresh off the block as a new Follower of Christ and this man comes with the story of Ruth. As we read together over the phone, we still had not met in person. I remember crying. I cried tears of joy, trembling even that God had moved suddenly in my love life. A man who fit my description to the T. On top of being tall, dark, and handsome as I mentioned earlier, he was also a powerful man of God who could lead me in this walk. He was kind, gentle; and talk about a thinker, this man had a good head on his shoulders.

He said he was family-oriented and simply needed a Kingdom wife. As overjoyed as I was, I was afraid that I would not be able to meet the expectations of being a Bishop's wife. I was not quite ready for that responsibility, so I ran. But the more I ran, the harder he chased me.

There was nothing I wanted that he did not provide; he made sure I was comfortable. We would talk for hours on the phone, with no dead air, just beautiful conversations. As we continued to speak over the phone, the deeper I fell.

He wanted to fly me in for lunch to his home state and fly me back the same day, but I would never do it. One day, he flew into my home state. We both were very pleased that we in person matched the description from the social media platform. Nervous as a sinner in church, I trembled as he stepped out of the car to open the door for me. He was such a gentleman from the moment we spoke years back.

We went to dinner, and I received a phone call from my then-best friend, she had recently had emergency surgery. I was so emotional at the dinner table and couldn't understand why she didn't call me to be there. My thoughts were, "What if she would have died?"

While sharing this with this gentleman, he yelled at me to let it go. I was blown away and asked him why he was so angry. He then asked if I was questioning him and became louder proclaiming I didn't honor him as a man. I was so confused, but to de-escalate the situation, I tried to apologize. He then slammed his cloth napkin on the table so hard the table shook. This was our first meeting, and I thought, "Where is the gentle giant I fell in love with who exhibited what I know now, the fruits of the spirit?"

I began to cry so hard.

I could not believe I was experiencing this from what I thought was a man of God. I ran out of the restaurant to get to the car to gather myself. I began questioning God... God is this you? Is this what your love feels like?

Moments later I could hear him fussing and carrying on as he walked back to the car. He was loud. Already embarrassed, I could not believe what was taking place. Is this real, is this happening, I thought. He gets in the car telling me I am disrespectful and that I did not respect his authority as a man. Crying even harder, he became louder in his scolding. Then he began to cry.

I was like whoa, what is this?

He was so sorry and fearful even as he said he was so afraid I would leave him, and he was right. I had never experienced a first date so crazy in my life. I recall thinking that this in no way from my walk, displayed the love of God.

Nevertheless, being who I am and learning what it was to be a Christ follower, I forgave Him. I mean Christ forgave me, right? In fact, it made me grow closer to him because I could see how someone had hurt him. Now I can see as I am sharing that I thought I was God and could save someone. I went as far as feeling the need to try and heal his hurt for him, I wanted to be his safe place. I was not Jesus, that was ***His*** job. But I would learn the hard way.

After we embraced each other, both expressing what seemed to be sincere apologies, I went with him back to his room. He was there only for one night, so we talked about what just happened. Just like that, this man was back in his gentleman mode for the rest of the night. We cuddled a bit but nothing beyond that. Never once did he make a move on me and trust me, we both were attracted to one another, but nothing happened. Not even a kiss on the lips. I was impressed and falling even further for this man.

Before he flew out, he was a full gentleman. He was back to opening doors, pulled out my chair, and as polite as ever. We had such an amazing end to our time together. It was like the day before had never happened. As if the drama we had experienced was a distant memory that would never return.

This was more like it.

I remember thinking to myself, okay this is God, I was just being tested, and I passed. What I know today is this was just the beginning of my troubles with this man. Had I known what I know today, I would have run to the hill which cometh my help and not just looked.

That devil is so cunning and my God, I wish I was better equipped to have seen it coming. That's why the Word encourages us to put on the whole armor that you may be able to stand against the schemes of the devil (**Ephesians 6**). Lord knows I had no clue about the armor of God, nor was I aware of the tricks of the enemy. I certainly was not aware of how to stand against the schemes of him or his minions. I was like fresh meat thrown in the middle of the ocean and the sharks smelled me a mile away and boy did they come running to attack.

As time went on, we continued our relationship. He insisted on flying me back and forth. He pampered me and wined and dined me for months. He literally spoiled me to the point that I wouldn't think twice about even looking at another man. I had found my Boaz and the monster on our first date, never returned. *"Satan himself is transformed into an angle of light,"* **2 Corinthians 11:14**.

I was in heaven, yup he had swept me off my feet. He would breakdown the Bible to me in a way that was so beautiful and quite attractive. I admired his knowledge in the word of God, and I believed God had sent me what I truly desired.

He had earned a doctorate in Theology, as well he had been given Honorary Doctorates of all kinds in Biblical studies, this man knew the word of the Lord. I was extremely grateful and honored that God sent me someone so powerful to help guide me in my new walk to prepare for His Kingdom. This encouraged me in many ways in this long-distance relationship with the bishop.

We spoke over the phone for hours, planning our lives together as he constantly reminded me, I could trust him so much. I would hang on to his every word, he is a man of God, and in my young believing mind he is perfect. He would not lead me wrong because God is leading him.

I became so absorbed with this man that I no longer had Bible study with my sisters. I would still listen to sermons online, but I wasn't going to the word myself. I wasn't seeking God for myself; I was instead seeking the bishop. I mean God did put him in my life, so in my mind, it was only right, right?

I could not have been more wrong.

Unfortunately, it took me years to realize that I had made this man my idol. God was not impressed nor was He pleased, but I had no way of knowing as I was not listening to the God of heaven, instead to the god of my chosen. Unbeknownst to me, this was the very thing God hated, putting other gods before Him (**Exodus 20:2-3**). It says, *"I am the Lord thy God, which have brought thee out of the land of Egypt, out of the house of bondage. Thou shalt have no other gods before me."*

This would not end well for me. God have mercy on my soul. As our relationship continued to develop, still long distance, this man became more obsessed with me and me with him. He became crazy with anyone, and I mean anyone that would say anything out of the way to me. If I reported it to him in casual conversation, he would deal with it in his way. That was ***not*** Yahweh.

At the time I did know that, however I thought it was his way of protecting me. I mean isn't that part of what a man would do for his woman. He moved me from where I was living into a loft in downtown Baltimore. It was beautiful, with cathedral ceilings, wooden floors, and a beautiful private yard for the kids. He furnished it with anything I needed because anything I shared with my ex-husband down to clothing; I had to get rid of. He simply would not allow his woman to have anything from another man, even if it was the father of her children.

There was absolutely nothing I wanted for emotionally, mentally or physically. I became sick a few days, and Bishop waited on me hand and foot. He was so gentle and so kind. He even paid my oldest to keep the youngest from disturbing my rest.

He had run to the car. I remember the girls being in their room, him in the kitchen, and suddenly, it happened. He came back proclaiming his love for me. He was in tears, got down at the side of my bed, pulled out a ring, and proposed. I was completely caught off guard, but I was over the moon with joy, so I said, "Yes."

My girls were laughing with joy because they were in on it. They were happy to see me happy.

I remembered working on my rideshare in the early mornings for extra money while I was working on my realtor's license. All he wanted me to do was study but allowed me to work the morning hours, on the condition that he had to be on the phone all the time. I thought this was cute, he loves me and is so protective, so I thought.

One day while on one of my routes, I didn't call him before leaving the house. He had been up the night before, so I wanted him to rest. He called me. Eager to hear his voice, I said, "Hey baby, good morning."

He asked, "Where are you?"

I let him know I was on the road with a passenger. You would have thought I said I was on a date with another man because oh boy, that did not go well. If he could have come through the phone, I truly believe he would have. He screamed through the phone that I was not to leave the house without telling him because there were crazy people out there and that he had to protect me. I tried to explain to him very calmly that I wanted him to rest. I also had a passenger so I needed to be considerate of my tone so they would not know I was upset. I would have thought this would have been understood by him. Instead, I tried to explain, but it only made things worse. He hung up the phone.

Trying to stay positive, my female passenger said to me, "Whatever that is you are in, get out of it."

I shared with her how much he loved me, how he is a Bishop, a man of God and just doesn't want to see me get hurt. This woman said, she knows because I am in love, it looks like its love, instead that was signs of an abuser. She shared a story of a relationship gone bad, and it started very similar to my situation. I said to her how sorry I felt for that person, but that was not my experience and would not be my portion. Besides he was sent by God.

The question then I should have been asking is which God he had been sent from. I could say it was the enemy, but it was the "inner me" who birthed this beast that was a saint in my eyes. Unknowingly, I was being groomed to idolize him instead of our Heavenly Father. Now I know that it was God using my passenger's words of wisdom to warn me that this relationship was not blessed by Him. I kept hearing her voice telling me that my man was broken, I deserved better. She begged me to get out before it was too late. That was the 1st time God sent me a lifeline to RUN. Unfortunately, I still lacked relationship with His son, as I was too focused on my relationship with this man.

Self-Reflection

Think of a time the Holy Spirit spoke to you in a warning that you may have ignored. How did it make you feel to know if you simply listened the first time, you could have avoided the consequences of your choices?

This is in no way to condemn you; it is instead to celebrate you as you have learned from that situation, and it is your testimony. Use the space below as well as the empty page provided if needed, to elaborate on that experience.

____

____

____

____

MEL SPEARS

Chapter 5

WOLF IN SHEEP'S CLOTHING

Matthew 7:15 says, *"Beware of false prophets, which come to you in sheep's clothing, but inwardly they are ravening wolves."*

Lauren Hill has a song called "Forgive Them Father." It says: *"It took me a little while to discover. Wolves in sheep clothing who pretend to be lovers, men who lack conscience will even lie to themselves. A friend once said, and I found to be true, that everyday people, they lie to God too. So, what makes you think that they won't lie to you? Forgive them father for they know not what they do."*

It wasn't until years later that I understood the Biblical correlation. Had I been in my word trying to please God, I may not have become so caught up in the world's religious titles or trying to please a man with a dark spirit. But how was I to know? He was a Bishop. I didn't quite know what the title Bishop entailed, I believed it meant the person was someone major in the eyes of God. There is no way someone with such a title would be so deceiving, right?

Wrong again.

At this point, no one has met this wonderful mystery man. My brother would joke about the idea that he was made up, just a figment of my imagination. Why hasn't anyone met him yet? One reason was the distance. When we **did** come together, it was for a short time. With both of us being divorced already, we didn't want the opinions of others to taint our concept of each other. He convinced me that we were all each other needed, and I was all for it.

Honestly, I could see brokenness in this man. I could see that someone hurt him badly. So, in my mind, in the same way, God had sent him to save me, God had, in turn, sent me to heal him. What I didn't understand at the time was that God had not done neither. This was not God, this was the work of Satan at best, and what a whirlwind of revelations I have now looked back on.

The enemy has a mission: **John 10:10** says, *"The thief cometh not, but for to steal, and to kill, and to destroy. I have come that they might have life and that they might have it more abundantly."*

This is not the journey 'man of God' was leading me on. As a new Follower of Christ, I wanted to believe otherwise all based on the idea of who he was as they had never met him. Again, I was oblivious. I didn't quite know what to expect from him being a Bishop other than knowing the Bible, he mastered that. But because I hadn't, I was like a lost sheep looking for a Shephard. Instead of him feeding his hungry sheep, he mishandled me. But it wasn't until later that God was truly revealing, again I missed it, but we will get there later.

***

It was Christmas and we were still living long distances from each other, the man of God stated he could not spend Christmas with me due to his daughter threatening to commit suicide. By this time, he had met and spent some time with my two girls and promised to spend Christmas with us. But because of this emergency, I understood. He then came two weeks later around my birthday time. At this point, I still had not met any of his family, not even his children. I asked if we could arrange to do so, I mean we were discussing marriage at this point, so I thought it was only right to at least meet his children.

Just to back up a little, I had been told that all his already 4 children were by the same woman who he had been divorced from for 6 years. So, I understood that after 20-plus years of marriage, it was still a sensitive thing for them who had grown up seeing their parents together and a very sensitive 6-year-old son. So, I was very forgiving and understanding, isn't that what Christ would do, forgive right?

Later, when I asked again for our children to meet, he became defensive, stating his children did not care to meet me. It was said in such a derogatory manner, but even then, I stayed hopeful. My God was I so naive. However, I did begin to pull back a little, and he noticed.

Valentine's Day he went over the top for my girls. Spoiling us was nothing new, however, this time had topped the others. He catered to me like never before as well as to my girls. I remember thinking, this is what happiness feels like.

After such a great day, Bishop asked me to ask my oldest daughter to keep my youngest in their room so he and I could spend time together. It was fine because we were all together during the day. Plus, he paid her, so my daughter was happy to do so. At the time, this notion seemed very cute and quite thoughtful, only this request became a thing. He'd even become irritated should he come to my home and the girls be in my room. Now that I think about it, it seemed Bishop did not want my children around me, and in a sense was trying to alienate my girls. This had become so bad that the girls would run into their room when he came in and out of town and knew he was close. When he left, I would rush them back into my room to be with me.

This went on for some time, but we had mastered it like a game. As I look back now, I cannot believe I allowed my girls to experience such madness. I can only attribute it to my head being so far in the clouds. Not so much now but, it seemed harmless because he showed he loved them in other ways and simply cared that I was not too overwhelmed with my children.

Winter had come to an end and spring was upon us. Bishop frequently traveled to and from what was told to me was his home state. It was great as I was comfortable with leaving the girls with their dad. It became so frequent; that he thought it be best I moved in. We were planning, I was super excited.

We had yet another amazing day together. That is until I received a call from my ex-husband concerning our daughter. Our daughter seemed to have some kind of allergic reaction. Unfortunately, my ex was not aware of what it may have been. Benadryl nor Motrin had helped at this point. Naturally, he became concerned, he wanted to take our daughter to seek medical attention.

Due to me having full custody, my ex would always seek after my advice and ask my opinion concerning our girl's health. I too agreed medical attention was necessary then I provided my children's father with the insurance information.

The bishop grunted and shifted himself on the chair we had been sitting on. Seeing his face as well as his body language, he was anything but pleased. I remember rubbing his hand and kissing his face a couple of times during the call to give assurance to him that this was not about me, but our children. This only backfired, as the more I tried to assure him; that this was nothing more than two parents working together for the wellness of our child, the angrier Bishop became.

By this time, he stood up and walked out. I remained still until I finished the call. Once off, I went to him with a sincere apology for how the call made him feel, assuring him once more that it was not about the two of us, but instead our child. All the discomfort and pressure I watched building up in him came out and it was forceful. He went into how my "baby daddy" wasn't a man, and how I was disrespectful to him even to take a call from a man in front of him. He proclaimed I didn't respect him and that he didn't have them issues with his "one" ex-wife of all his children. Well, I found out later that was one of his many lies.

I'll go into that further.

I began to cry as I tried to explain to him why my ex called even though he could hear the conversation. My goal was to put him at ease. Instead of me being able to explain, he accused me of cheating along with all kinds of wicked things. I was in pure disbelief this was coming from the bishop, a man of God, *my* man. The one who said he loved me and would never hurt me.

At that time, I was oblivious that someone in Christ who knew the word so well could act like this. I wasn't aware the Bible had warned of this type of person/spirit coming in sheep's clothing but inside was a ravaging wolf. Sadly, it had become World War III in a matter of seconds in that once quite peaceful and loving home. He stood over me with pure anger in his eyes. For the 1st time, I was afraid of this man. I was there alone in another state, and no one knew my exact location or who I was with.

I ran upstairs, my spirit said, "Get out!!"

That's what I was doing. I was getting out! I packed up everything I could to catch the next flight home. I was afraid for my life, he was slamming and throwing things, and I didn't want to be next. I was trembling in fear, and this man displayed no self-control. He burst into the room telling me I was not leaving him.

He grabbed my bags, we tussled and suddenly, this 6'3" man was crying like a baby, falling to the floor. He cried like never before. He told me how much of a failure he was, how he believed what his mother said about him, that he would never be anything, and that everyone would leave him because he couldn't be loved.

No longer did I see him as a threat but the bruised young boy who had yet to heal. My heart broke for him as a mothers would for her child, and a wife for her husband. Aren't I supposed to be his help mate? How could I leave him like this? I got down on the floor with him promising I wouldn't leave. We cried together, cleaned ourselves up, and went for a beautiful dinner.

I could hear what I know now to be the Holy Spirit, that I needed to go. But I didn't have enough confidence in what I was hearing vs what I was seeing. I struggled with the thought of leaving, but how can I leave this man so fragile like this and call myself a Christian?

Well, I stayed at least a week longer. We had amazing times together that week. He made me breakfast in bed, cooked me dinner, and waited on me hand and foot. We shopped, went to church, and just had a wonderful time. He simply needed to be loved, and I was the one to love him.

The day before I was to leave, out of nowhere I was yelled at because I was too nice, he said. "You smile too much; everyone doesn't need to see your teeth."

I was so confused, what was wrong with this man I thought. We are having an amazing week; how could we be right back to him yelling and screaming at me about cheating on him? This was not in my character; I tried to plead with him and let him know how much I loved him. I cried, I begged, I would never cheat on you, but it was not enough. It continued for so long that I was exhausted from crying at this point, but I gathered enough strength to go and pack.

He then ran behind me banging on the door; this was a repeat from the last time. Only this time I am leaving because I'm done. I did not open the door this time and it was locked. A few moments after it went quiet outside the door, I heard a loud thump, a fall even. I was concerned more about him than me at this point. I knew he had guns in the house, I didn't hear a gunshot, but I was praying that wasn't what caused the sound of him possibly falling.

I ran downstairs to find Bishop on the floor holding his chest and looking to be almost lifeless. I rushed to him in tears, placing his head in my lap. I began dialing 911, he jumped up saying that he was ok and laughed.

I cried in anger.

How could someone play like that? I went back upstairs to finish packing. "He said you're going to leave me, right? Well, go ahead. My mother was right anyway, no one loves me, no one stays."

Again, I gave in, we canceled my flight, and I stayed another few days before going home. At this point, he needed to travel to Florida to see his young son. He was gone for several days, which was fine because I had the huge house to myself and he called me daily, even allowing me to speak with his son. I was so in awe of the kind of person he portrayed himself to be. I felt something when he wouldn't answer directly when I called but always called me back right away.

While at the airport, I remember us having a great conversation, until he heard a male talking in the background. He asked who I was talking to. I told him someone was just making small talk about our flight. The Mr. went off on me over the phone. The more I tried to calm him, the more enraged he became. He was convinced I was trying to talk to this man as if we planned to be at the airport together. He hung up the phone in my ear and I just cried.

At this point, I had made up my mind that I would not come back, I was done. There was no reasoning with this man, whatever he believed to be so was just that. I could not take this anymore. I immediately blocked his phone, each of them, and deleted all our texts as well as his numbers.

I boarded the plane; I felt closure began to take place. With the distance between us, I could now pick up my life. I went back to being my own boss and paying my own way again. I set a goal to buy another car as my previous one was totaled out. I was looking forward to seeing my girls and sleeping in my own bed.

By the time I had landed, I noticed I had tons of voice messages. Concerned they were from my children, I checked them right away. My God, it was him, over 16 messages. The first few just hung up, the others gradually became worse.

I recall one voice message was the bishop screaming, "YOU BLOCKED ME, YOU BLOCKED ME!" The last couple messages were him crying, "No one loves me." And the last message he asked, "How could you block me?" he cried, "I have been nothing but good to you." He cried further, "Please unblock me."

I was wondering if there were different people on my voice messages. What I believe now is multiple personalities were being displayed in those messages, personalities of an unstable person (just my opinion).

I was determined not to cave into his tricks of crying and playing the victim again. I began going deeper into God's word but working all kinds of crazy hours because I would no longer have access to the lifestyle this man was providing. I couldn't afford to continue staying in this downtown loft, with new vehicle and insurance, etc. Unless I planned to work extra hard to keep it, yes that's what I intended to do. I had never been afraid of hard work; in fact it's the other half of my life story.

But it was so good to have had a small break from having to work as hard, due to Bishop's generosity.

Unfortunately, the price I had to pay for that lifestyle was not worth it. As I think back, I believe my lack of need to be independent and being dependent on the bishop was all in his plan.

I recall receiving notifications of large payments through an app on my phone. I knew immediately where the funds had come from. He had stopped calling but he still followed through on his commitment to handle my bills. I was moved by the bishop's nice gesture in keeping his word. Nevertheless, this did not stop my grind as I wasn't sure when the other side of him might show up again and possibly stop him from continuing.

While out working, I received a call from a strange number a few times, I allowed it to go to voice mail. The last time the caller left a voice message. It was the bishop's brother, so he said. Later I would find out differently. Please note that other than his young son, I had not met nor spoken to any of his family. Again, there was no big deal because outside of my girls, it was only due to them living with me, nor had he met any of my family. So, to hear this voice message from someone stating he was the bishop's brother asking me to please call due to urgency I became worried and called.

I dialed the number trembling, worried something had happened, praying there was no bad news. He answered, immediately sharing with me the family's concern involving Bishop. He was not eating, drinking, or leaving the house, Bishop was falling into a depression. The brother begged for forgiveness on the bishop's behalf. Even agreeing that he can be passionate about what he stands for. We laughed and he said, "Please give my brother a call. He loves you so much, and I don't know him to love anyone as much he loves you. I certainly hope to meet you someday."

This is now mid to late June, and it is hot outside, sitting in my car with AC, I decided to call Bishop. Immediately, he broke down crying, "I'm sorry," I too began to cry. I told him how scary he was. How I am uncertain of what I will get when he goes off on me, that us being together is not a good idea. He cried harder and hung up the phone. I cried too but I knew I needed to stand my ground.

"This man is unstable," I thought.

I still had not unblocked him, but I received another call from his brother. "Sis, please give him another chance, just hear him out so he can stop calling me crying. I don't want to hear it."

We both laughed. I agreed I would unblock the bishop. A call came in right away, this time a calm, clear, and focused voice came across my phone. Bishop stated to me how he had called everyone and realized where he had gone wrong. He expressed how embarrassed and deeply sorry he was for acting as he had on multiple occasions. He proclaimed he disappointed God and those he loved. I have to say, there were red flags due to his previous behavior, but I'd be lying if I said his words did not move me.

And so, I did what I thought was God saying to forgive him. What I know now that I didn't know then is, forgiveness does not necessarily mean access. Nevertheless, I was touched by his willingness to take full responsibility for his actions to not just me but others concerning me. He even told me his brother (the one who called me) as well as his father told him he was a fool and to get me back to make things work with me. Can you imagine, a man I never met, the dad of this man I thought I loved, corrected him on my behalf? I was so moved I believed we had a fighting chance. Boy, was I wrong but you could not tell me this at that time.

Looking back, what I would have told myself was to listen to the quiet still voice which was the Holy Spirit speaking. I was not spiritually mature enough to know to fight in the spirit through prayer at the time so I simply should have stayed away. Sometimes trying to help others will ultimately hurt us. That is not God's plan. The word says, love your neighbor as you love yourself. The key to that for me is you must first know how to love yourself otherwise, you will not know how to truly love others.

Have you ever had this experience or one similar where you see all the red flags of a situation whether it be a relationship, friendship, workship, kinship, etc., yet you continue to try to help, even though it is hurting you? Pause for a moment and think about how you responded then, maybe being new in your faith vs how you may respond now.

Use the space below as well as the empty page provided if needed, to elaborate on that experience.

Chapter 6

TIL DEATH DO US PART...

Within months, we were married, at least I thought. Also with child, my girls are in our beautiful new home with my Boaz. It was an amazing time with him. We had no more fights, he took care of everything, we wanted for nothing.

One week before my birthday the pregnancy was confirmed by an at home pregnancy test. I noticed a shift in the bishop. He looks confused and I immediately regretted the pregnancy. I literally fell to the floor crying. Surprisingly, Bishop came over comforting me with love. He told me this is not a bad thing, instead a blessing. He promised we would get an even bigger house than we already had, and I would have an amazing pregnancy with him right by my side.

That weekend I found him coming in later and leaving more frequently. The same happened around Christmas the month before, but he assured me it was just work. I had a dream that he was murdered in his line of work. He claimed he was some sort of Marshall going state to state to bring in fugitives. He had all sorts of guns and badges, so I understood. However, I was not convinced that was the only reason.

Again, his behavior shifted.

Bishop became very distant from the girls and me. He ate dinner separately from us and all. Months before the girls moved in, I would wake out of my sleep to go into the living room to pray. He was not happy about that. It seemed the closer I became to God, the further he came from me, again many signs to leave but I didn't.

So here we are pregnant.

Out of the blue, Bishop offers to make me a "healthy" smoothie. I'm only a few weeks pregnant so I understand his desire to make sure the baby is growing healthy. I recall the girls and I sitting in the living room which allowed us to see into our huge open kitchen. I walked into the kitchen, immediately being told by Bishop to get out in a loving way. But this raised an eyebrow, and I jokingly asked what he was putting into my smoothie. He laughed, kissed me and patted my butt to escort me out.

As I walked out, I remembered what seemed to be him putting something in the trash. Only this wasn't the typical way of throwing something in the trash, he lifted trash that was already there to strategically put what he had to trash under what was already there. I thought no more of it and soon my smoothie was ready, and it was hand delivered to me as I rested on our plush sofa.

Before I could take a sip, my little girl asked me to taste it. Bishop looked angry from what I learned later, was fear. I finished my smoothie that Bishop insisted on making for me the one he was bothered that my baby was asking to sip, and he left, and the girls and I relaxed.

A few moments later, the Holy Spirit told me to go lift the trash and see what was in it. I was weak when I saw what was in there. It was six packs of stand back powder to try and abort our very early pregnancy. I ran to the bathroom sick to my stomach from what was being downloaded to me. I was angry, sad, hurt, and so many emotions were going through me.

Why would he do that? I thought we were happy. I cried so hard in disbelief. Even with what the Holy spirit was showing me, I thought there must be some sort of explanation. I prayed and still wasn't obedient.

I thought those packs were old that he himself had taken over time for his shoulder injury. Holy Spirit said no, but I had to confirm. I called Bishop several hours later asking him how his arm was feeling. He stated it was better, no pain. I was saddened because he had not been taking anything. But I asked him anyway, I just needed to hear it for myself.

"Is it better because you are taking pain medication?"

He said, "No baby, its good, I haven't had to take anything."

I am now afraid my baby as well as myself are in danger.

Again, the Holy Spirit told me to RUN. I secretly sought after help. He controlled the finances so he would know if I took a lump of money to leave. I had nowhere to go and didn't know what to do. I am pregnant and have two other kids under 15. What was I to do? I couldn't tell too much, who would believe me that he is trying to kill my baby. I have no proof. Besides he is connected to the mayor and all kinds of government officials, he may try to kill me. So, I was careful how I moved and what I said to others about the situation.

But something happened.

Bishop was back to being the super amazing guy I know him to be. Again, I began to question what I was feeling about the whole situation, I knew it was the Holy Spirit but maybe I heard something wrong. Maybe it was me. Maybe he had not taken meds recently but maybe that was from some time before. I was truly talking myself out of what I know now was so clear instruction to leave.

When not secure in your relationship with Christ, you will question the voice of God, overriding the Holy Spirit. Thankfully for me, in my ignorance God was protecting me when I don't know I needed to be protected. I eventually told Bishop what I was feeling. That I thought he was trying to kill our baby or hurt me. I gave him all the details. He looked like he saw a ghost, yet he still denied it.

He broke down crying, asking me how I could accuse him of such. His baby girl died in his arms some time ago and he hadn't gotten over it. He said he would never hurt his child. Relieved, I must have been wrong, I sat on his lap wrapping my arms around him now also in tears and apologizing for accusing him of such dark things. Everything was well until it wasn't.

Again, I am now being waken up out of my sleep around 3:00 AM each night. One night I was in the living room praying. He walked in upset that I got out of bed leaving him there. He stated angrily, "Oh, I guess you are praying again?" He shook his head and stormed back to the room.

I just cried asking God what to do. Mind you, I was already warned to leave, I didn't take heed to it and now, thinking about it, I was very disobedient. I thought I could fix him. He just needs love. Making love was different, harder more aggressive and he would go much longer. So, I knew he wasn't cheating because Bishop could not take his hands off me.

I found myself running in many instances, he was too aggressive. The girl's drifted further from him, Bishop was like a dark cloud. I wanted to fight; I needed my marriage to work.

He was now accusing me of cheating, back to yelling and throwing things around the house. He slammed every door he walked through. Again, I was afraid. To avoid sleeping with him, I would do rideshare at night, I also needed the money.

I would tell my oldest to keep her sister in her room and lock the door. Their rooms were upstairs, they had the entire upstairs, so he never went up there. I was glad because this man once again is really scaring me. I must get out.

One morning when I was heading back from trying to seek help to get out, he called saying he was headed to his surgery, and his male assistant was taking him. In that moment it was an eerie feeling coming over the phone. I just wanted out, so I simply ignored it. I did not know it would be one of the last times I would hear from him.

About an hour later he called again telling me he never meant to hurt me, and he had never loved anyone as much as he loved me. He said in the next breath in and angry voice, "You're trying to keep my child away from me, aren't you?"

I was alarmed and scared because I didn't know what he knew. We ended the call for his outpatient surgery. Only that indeed was the last time I would hear his voice, and my child would never meet his father.

The next call that came in was around 3:00 PM and I was told Bishop died in surgery. I was grateful but afraid at that time but what I know now is God was doing what I didn't have the strength to do. He protected me from unseen and seen danger. This man was not mentally stable and my need to fix him kept me in what I now know was mental and emotional abuse. But thank God that He protects fools and babies. I don't know which I was more of, maybe both.

In a matter of hours, I found out I was not legally married to this man. The family he told me was his family was not true. Not the brother, nor the father who He claimed wanted him to fight for me. And get this, not only had he been married previously, but he was also still married to his son's mother. Not to mention he had four other children by four other women. I was sick to my stomach and I felt violated.

What was it all for? He chased me for two years only to bring me into a web of deceit as I later found out his previous marriage ended because he had an affair with his current wife. I thought I would lose my mind.

He was not a Marshall, he did not work for the mayor's office, and he was not even from the state he told me he was from. It was all a lie, and he is no longer here so I can't even confront him. I believe now God took him as He had me in the book of Jeremiah in the Bible concerning Shepherds misleading the sheep. I was too naive to see it then, but I see it now. Unfortunately, some of us don't learn from our experiences and until we do, we will have to repeat it, stay tuned.

You will see it later in the chapter.

As for now, back then I was so young in my faith. As I sat at that time and processed what was happening during the past few seasons of my life: my unborn child's father passes, learning he has a high chance of Trisomy 21 (Down Syndrome), and my mom passing. Then I learned I was losing my house, lost my car and was in a moment of losing my mind.

I had no one to turn to, I was in a state far from home, just my girls, myself and my unborn baby. I began to wonder what it is all for and why anyone would want to live through this. I remember the enemy saying to me, "Where is your God now? You choose to serve Him and He leaves you."

For a moment I believed the enemy, I believed I was all alone. I sat on the floor, and I began to cry as I contemplated ending it all. I didn't know how or when; I was just convinced it was necessary. As I sulked in tears, I remembered that soft still voice whisper, "I am here, I have not left you."

That was the first time I remembered **Proverbs 3:5,7**, *"Trust in the Lord, with all your heart, lean not to your own unborn; acknowledge me in all your ways and He will make your path straight."*

I smiled so hard, as my tears of sorrow turned from sadness to joy. I jumped up off the floor and began to praise God, thanking Him, not for just my unborn child, but also for failing to attempt to end my life. Had I been successful in committing suicide, I would have ended the life of my unborn too. Immediately, I repented and instantly I could feel I was forgiven. I had such confidence in it that I felt much lighter, just as if it never had happened.

As I walked into the kitchen, I noticed a red bird outside the window. I had never seen a bird in the yard and not one in the window, so I became curious. I googled red bird. I was amazed by the findings. It indicated angels are near when you see a Red Bird (Cardinal). I smiled with such joy in my heart as I believed this was true. I don't believe much in Google all the time, but something about an angel being near, rung true for me.

Self-Reflection

Can you recall a time when you believed you were finally able to breathe? You felt able to breathe, yet your breath seems to be taken away due to life events that have their hands around your throat? How did Jesus send you a reminder of His love, just when you thought it was over?

Use the space below as well as the empty page provided if needed, to elaborate on that experience. What's a scripture of prayer you may turn to?

____

____

____

____

____

____

____

____

____

____

____

____

____

____

____

Chapter 7

SPINACH & CARROT

Like most women, my body was going through what I thought was a change due to my age. Life was Life'ing as it often does so it was almost expected that with age and the stressor of everyday living, my hormones would be wacky.

So, I wasn't too worried when my cycle did not show for a month. I knew I was not pregnant; it just wasn't humanly possible. Well, I guess it could be possible with all the resources available, but since I had not tapped into any of those resources, it wasn't possible. That took me back to the changes in hormones due to stress, aging, etc. I figured it would be back to normal the next month, besides my cycle was never what most would consider normal.

This was all part of the process.

As I had imagined my cycle did eventually come. I had always been one of the few women who was excited about "Aunt Flow" flowing. Only this time, it had been a full month since she had visited. So, seeing her this month was nothing short of special for me. I celebrated, yes, I did. Again, not out of fear of pregnancy but the uncertainty of my health.

I ordered crab cakes, had a glass of wine, and even had dessert, I mean Aunt Flow was flowing, so to me this meant I am a woman, hear me roar. And that's what I did. A week went by, then another, another then another, and Aunt Flow was still here. My cycle that went from being missing a whole month has now decided to stay a full month with what looked like no end.

Just as missing my cycle for one month wasn't a thing I had experienced, nor was this. So, I figured, okay the same is taking place here with the extended flow as it did with the lack of flow. Hormones, I thought, yup that's it. Flow was out of wack, and I seemed to become weaker by the day. My body was exhausted, I was losing what seemed like gallons of blood, well at least to me it felt like gallons. I was sleeping a lot and honestly began to worry. Even more now than I did with no flow. I began to speak with other women who shared similar situations. Many of whom had suggested it had to be that my uterus needed to be removed due to all kinds of things.

This frightened me. I am not one that likes to have anything I was born with removed from my body, so this cycle thing needed to get a grip on itself, so I didn't have to have any type of surgery. I had heard many women who were happy to have it gone, the uterus that is, which the medical term is "hysterectomy." A full or partial removal was the going thing for most I knew as it meant no more irregular cycles, in all actuality, it meant no more cycles period (no pon intended) nor any babies. Well, I was okay with the no baby thing, but I was not okay with no cycle, again, it was the one thing that reminded me that I indeed am woman. Of course, it wasn't the only thing but indeed one of them that distinguished women from men.

After still seeing my cycle now for a second month, I began to really wonder about the fibroid I had been diagnosed with that always seemed to flare up during pregnancy, only again, I was not pregnant, what is happening.? I'm losing too much blood.

I attempted to make an appointment with my gyno doctor because this is from what I'm told very dangerous. With little to no energy and losing so much blood, I knew this was the truth. But I also knew I didn't want my uterus removed. I have three blessings in children form from God, but I knew I was still so young and what if my husband to be wanted more? I just couldn't believe that God would take my womb from me.

I remember scheduling with my gyno, but the appointment was so far out, I just didn't understand. I thought, "Did they want me to bleed out?" But then I remembered the woman with the issue of blood. She had bled twelve years, and I could not imagine what her life had been like. I'm sure she had insecurities, weakness, lack of acceptance and was cast out by many because according to the Bible when a woman is on her cycle, she is unclean. I don't recall the Bible saying such, but I don't believe she was married or had any children. Her uterus was malfunctioning.

So, I thought, "I have been married, have children, so maybe God doesn't have any further use of my uterus. My issue had nothing on this woman in the Bible I mean she bled for years, mine at this point were a measly 2.5 months."

How dare I believe what the enemy was saying to me? Even after all she endured, this woman believed in the power of Jesus so much that she didn't let nothing stop her from getting to him. She knew that if she could only touch the hem of His garment, because getting through the crowd to get access to Him was almost impossible, so just the hem of His garment would be sufficient that she indeed would be healed. That is a faith that is so great, she believed that the anointing of Jesus Christ was so powerful that it would even penetrate His garments.

As the story in the book of Luke unfolded, it spoke on Jesus asking who touched Him, again it wasn't even Him she touched but His clothing, but her faith was so powerful that it pulled from Jesus. When you go to **Luke 8**, the scripture tells us that this woman had spent all her living on the word of man, doctors, physicians etc. But it wasn't until she spoke the words *"If I could only touch the hem of his garment,"* that she knew she would be healed.

And it was so. This notion made me so excited; to know we can have such bold faith that can pull the very virtue from our Christ Jesus because of the power of the word that we have been given. Can you imagine what that same faith in God can do when it comes to suppressing the enemy?

Well, I put it to work, instead of leaning on what others may have experienced or said to me, no matter what the doctors may have even said. I needed to believe in what God said about me. **Philippians**

4:11 says, *"I can do All things through Christ Jesus that strengthens me."*

That next day, the Holy Spirit had me research carrots and spinach. I didn't quite know why, all I knew was I was still weak and bleeding heavily. I looked up spinach and carrots online and to my surprise, they both were said to aid in the issues with the uterus. Now I believed what the powers of trusting in God could do, but there was no way a carrot and some spinach would fix this problem.

But my God, the Holy Spirit almost pushed me out of the bed and had me go to my refrigerator. I don't know when I purchased spinach or carrots, however, I had both in my fridge. That was mind blowing for me. The Holy Spirit had me clean and put them both in my ninja with just coconut water. At this point, I was still trusting God, but not man and figured eventually because of my faith like the woman with the issue of blood, I would too be healed. So, out of obedience I drank the concoction.

Shortly after, with every breath in me, I went to the restroom as normal, preparing for a huge clean up and proper preparation. My flow had been coming out of my clothes, and this type of preparation had been my practice for the past two months and a half and I was certain this would be the case at this time. Well to God be the Glory, not only was there no huge mess to clean up, but there was also nothing dropping in the toilet. This blew my mind because the heavy bleeding was drying up right before my eyes. As the day went on, the blood had stopped completely. It wasn't drying up, it was gone. I was blown away by the blood of Christ and my faith in Him. It wasn't the spinach nor the carrots that were the healing components that healed me in just a day, instead it was my *obedience* in moving according to what the Holy Spirit had instructed me to do. Most importantly, my faith to comply. Had I not had faith in the word, which is Christ Jesus, I would not have been able to be obedient to the action of the resources, the source our Heavenly Father allowed to be put in place to heal me.

As of today, I have no other issues with blood, I did however have an issue with my gallbladder. Like before, the same rules applied unlike what I did prior with the health scare or what the woman with the issue of blood did prior to her faith. I immediately activated the powers within that had been given to me by the renewing of my mind in Christ Jesus.

See what happens is often we will have the same test in our lives and just like in the education system, in the University of Christ, if we fail the test, we may have to repeat that same test. Thankfully because of the love of Christ, we are equipped to win. We must simply tap into the source who is God not what the enemy says.

When we do, any diagnosis or problems we may receive will be defeated as well as the enemy and we indeed win.

Because of my faith, I no longer needed surgery as the doctors so urgently stated I would. Instead, when I returned for a follow-up appointment, there was no sign of any issue with my gallbladder. Did we make the doctors out to be liars? Absolutely not because it was there previously. But because of my faith, it overpowered the presence of sickness, and it had to flee. I activated the 'resources' from the source, spoke to that mountain and it was indeed moved. **Mark 11:23**.

Self-Reflection

Is there anything too hard for God? Not according to his word.

I'd like you to take this time and pause, think of something in your health that may seem to be causing you pain or discomfort. Place your hand on that area and ask the Holy Spirit if there is anything you can do to reverse that illness or suffering, no matter how silly it may seem. Listen, it could be something as simple as changing your food choices.

Please share your experience. Use the space below as well as the empty page provided if needed, to elaborate on that experience.

____

____

____

____

____

____

____

____

____

____

____

____

____

____

____

____

Chapter 8

TAKE UP YOUR CROSS

My beautiful son was born 8 lbs. 9 oz and 20 inches long, yet he was still three weeks early. Throughout my pregnancy, I knew this child was special.

The summer before He was conceived, the Holy Spirit had me in the book of Jeremiah, it wasn't until later that I would find out why. I remember still getting up daily to do ride share in my early weeks of pregnancy. It was the only time I could cry and be alone with the Lord without the girls seeing me upset.

Losing his dad to a heart attack at only six weeks into the pregnancy was devastating, yet somehow a relief. I'm sure you understand due to what I shared in previous chapters. Good, bad or indifferent, the pain ran deep. I cared deeply for him and only wished he had received therapy for his childhood hurts and pains that poured into his adulthood. Besides, he was still my unborn child's father, the thought of my son coming into this world not ever being able to see his father was devastating. Therefore, leaving out extra early to cry was my only way to truly express that hurt.

So, before each ride in the early hours of the morning, I would sit in my car and just cry. I was strong for my girls as they too were grieving, during conversations with family members and friends I stayed strong as well. I never liked others to see me come off as if I was weak, so I would hold it together.

Apparently, I held it together too well as I had a close cousin at the time speculate to others that I must have had something to do with the death of my unborn child's father. So, on top of trying to hold it together after such a lost, I had to hear from others that this "woman of God" is stating that there is no way a "healthy man" would just die from a heart attack. This was due to her opinion of me not doing enough to investigate what happened. What she failed to realize, and I didn't bother to explain, is God had shown me in a dream just weeks prior an injury bishop had experienced in his shoulder. Though it scared me that there would be a death, I wasn't aware the death would be physical. I did warn him at that time, but he was certain of a promise he believed God gave to him, that he would live to be very old. That must have been in dog years as he was barely 50. But that's beside the point. May he rest in peace.

Anyway, all of this was just too much for me and my unborn child, so I could not wait until the early morning as I needed to get it out. Nights would have been a great time as well to cry out to the Lord, only the kids slept in my bed, so they were up under me all day. My only option was to cry in the car before my first passenger, otherwise I would have been a wreck when my girls were around or even with my passengers in the car.

Surprisingly, my car became my war room if you will and it also became sort of therapeutic for me. This time allowed me to talk to the Holy Spirit. I let God know how I angry I was that this left me lonely, yet thankful and confident that I was not alone. I cried, prayed, rejoiced, and worshipped each morning.

One of those mornings, I did not feel like going out but I was so thankful that I had. My very first passenger was an older woman. She got into my car close to one of the train stations where I lived. At this point, it wasn't even 5:30 am. Naturally, I had on my mask of happiness to disguise the pain, so we began to talk. This was normal for me during ride share as I am a people's person and it was a great way to take my mind off things at home. As emotional and as difficult as those moments were leading up to my first morning pick-up, God would always give me the strength to press forward as no matter what, I still had to share how good He had been to me.

I remained positive with my riders. As normal, the conversation was about the love of Jesus and even in this, I knew He was there. I spoke about how blessed I was to be pregnant. From there unbeknownst to this woman, God had already told me to name my baby. Too early for the sex of the baby to be revealed, I was given the name of this precious baby in my womb. Be it girl child or boy, I knew I would be obedient.

Surprisingly, this passenger who I had never met nor spoken to me, stated, "It's a boy."

As shocked as I was, I was so confident she was correct. As there was no way she could have known, again I had not yet had it confirmed. I began to cry, and I remembered this day so clearly because I was unable to move, I could only cry. A few minutes felt like forever before I could drive. It began to rain, hard. Between my tears and the rain, I could barely see clearly. But I continued to drive, slowly as I spoke to God and this woman ministered to me.

It was as if God Himself took over the wheel for me. The sun had not yet risen, but the Risen Son had sent the comforter for me through this woman. She must have been a prophet. God sent her to minister to me in such a way telling me that this boy child I was carrying already had an anointing on his life and how God was intentional in giving him to me, that he is my gift. She reminded me that God sees my tears and loved me. I cried hard in praise thanking God for thinking so much of me. When I stopped the car, I don't even remember doing so, this woman got out went up a hill and vanished. I could no longer see her. I know today, she was my angel.

After that day, the cries were different. No longer a sad cry, more of a joyous and celebratory cry. I was certain that I had been forgiven for my role in being disobedient. A peace came over me that I never would have imagined. I now had the courage to go forward, I couldn't clearly see the hand of God upon my life, yet our Heavenly Father knew I needed a special word that day and I received it.

A few months later, my mother was gravely ill in the hospital. Prior to learning of the pregnancy and before the death of the father, I purchased tickets to see a well-known Bishop in person in Florida, and I intended to still go. In fact, Holy Spirit made it possible that I could go even after my tragic loss.

Only days before the event, I received word that my mom was gravely ill in the hospital, and this was another weight I had to bear during my pregnancy. I just could not understand. I had just finished mourning the death of my son's father, how is it God would now allow another death before I can finish bringing my son into this world?

I could not comprehend this, being four months pregnant. I was losing my mom, my girls are taking another hit, losing their grandmother and yet another person my unborn son will not be blessed to meet as they both are leaving before, he enters the world. I was devasted and I wondered how this could be God. Nevertheless, I still trusted.

I prepared for my trip to Florida which was supposed to include spiritual rejuvenation as well as some relaxation. It's now possibly a trip to say goodbyes to my mom. She too was in the Florida area so I was strategic in renting a car to be sure I could see my mom before the spiritual event. I just knew I could not miss either.

I believed there was a message with me there and possibly the last time I'd see my mom alive. I finally arrived at the hospital after flying to where the event was then drove another two hours. During that drive, I prayed and worshiped in the name of Jesus. I believed with the presence with the Lord upon me, my mom would have a fighting chance. I was confident that if simply pray and trust, death would pass my mom like all the other times before. In my mind, all would be well with my mom.

My posture slightly changed once I reached her room as I was not prepared for what I saw. I was so used to my mom being so strong, only this time was not the case. My mother was non-responsive, I felt weak and cried out to God.

I prayed "God please don't take my mom."

I was fearful he would but confident He would deliver on my request. I prayed, and I believed. Days later my mom's health continued to decline, so we needed to make a decision as a family. This is not what I was used to with my mom, she was a survivor, and she was the first savior I referenced even into my adulthood. She overcame child molestation, rejection from her mom who allowed her adult brother to rape my mom on various occasions. My mother also survived drug addiction, domestic violence, alcoholism, two aneurysms that burst, ultimately taking her vision. Yet she continued to fight and enjoy life, in fact my mom would dance her pains away, no matter what was going on, she would dance.

Only this time, the music had stopped, and the dance had ended; my mother had no more fights in her. As much as I prayed, the worse her condition became. We were torn without a decision; it was becoming clear that maybe it was time for her eternal rest. I took my mom's hand, letting her know we would fight to keep her alive, but only if that was what she wanted. I asked her to squeeze my hand if she wanted to stay on life support and there was nothing, however a tear rolled down her cheek. I then asked her to squeeze my hand if she was ready to go home with the Lord. She squeezed my hand and even raised her eyebrows. It was clear to me, but unfortunately, her sister was not in agreement.

I told her I trust God; my mother's life was in God's hands. I believed that His will would be done. My mother's sister felt that meant I was giving up on my own mom. That hurt, and yet again, my faith in God was a reflection to a family member meant I was pulling the trigger. It hurted as it reminded me of what my cousin had been insinuating concerning my son's late father. Instead, I was simply giving in to His will not mine. I was at peace whichever way it would go.

More family flew in.

Once my sister arrived, we agreed to take our mom off the breathing machine. We were warned she would not survive through the night; I trusted God. My mother's breathing slowed; she was dying right before my eyes. To make the transition more comfortable, we moved her to hospice as we all agree that she was at peace with transitioning. Besides, we did not want our mom to suffer living on a life machine as a vegetable.

I trusted God.

Mom was cleaned up beautifully and made comfortable for her peaceful departure. I kissed my mom and said my final goodbyes to her and comforted my sister after praying and I left. There was an assignment for me on the other side of Florida, two hours away.

My family was not pleased. At the time I was reminded of the disciple who said he would follow Christ after he buried his dad. Most would make that same request thinking Jesus would comply. Only Jesus in so many words declined his request and simply stated, *"Let the dead, bury the dead."*

For me, that meant if I am going to follow Christ, I could not allow the circumstances, or even the death of a loved one, not even my mom, to interfere. It was a difficult choice, but I needed to decide, and I did despite the ridicule from my family. I picked up my cross and I followed Christ.

During the Spiritual event, I had a miraculous breakthrough in my life concerning my children. The Holy Spirit spoke so clearly through the speakers in the panels, and I was blessed. It prepared me for the future storm to come. Does that mean had I stayed with my mom, I would not have received it? Not necessarily as God has already predestined what's for me. However, it was the practice of obedience in that difficult time which was necessary to fully receive it.

We are given free will, we can do it our way, but God's way is always best. The word says obedience is greater than sacrifice; obedience won, and so did I. I wanted to be with my mother at her last breath, but I wanted more to be pleasing to my

Savior. This reminded me of the story in the Bible when Jesus was notified that his mom and brothers wanted to speak with him. Jesus knew he had a mission and could not allow the people of the world to keep him from it. He asked them who is my mother and brothers. He was speaking about his kingdom siblings being his family, those who died to the will of the Father. When we are called, we must answer, despite what people think or feel as they were not the ones who died for our sins.

This was my test allowed by the Lord: would I be more focused on the things in this world or instead focus on His words? It's never an easy decision, especially when it comes to family or loved ones. But I knew I needed to choose wisely.

Can you relate to this experience? What's your go to scripture in times like this? Please take a moment to reflect on those times and take the space on the next page to share your own experience.

Chapter 9

SEASONS OF CHANGE

It seems from what I have picked up from conversations with others is most relationships fail due to the relationship becoming stale in a sense, or the desires of one or both in the marriage change, increase or are no longer desired. We as human beings are constantly evolving, shouldn't change be expected in our relationships? Unfortunately, some of us aren't willing or possibly aware of when it's time to change. Not just for your partner but as well as for yourself.

Many retail stores and some other businesses have semi-annual sales. I believe this is because they are aware that seasons change, as we do. As the season changes, so does what we wear, eat and do. Sometimes change is sudden, other times it happens over the years. This could be due to the change in our age, education, environment, relationship with God, etc.

The same goes for our marriages. But unlike what we do in marriage, these companies recognize the change, often from paying attention to their customers, doing surveys and of course great research. How else would they know that January and June are a great time for that change? The company does not close the stores, end the contract or give up.

So, why do we?

Why can't we, like these companies, invest more into our spouses? Why do we lack so much grace when it comes to the one who we promised God we would spend our lives with? Granted, there are some marriages that were not ordained by God, but that is not the conversation here, I am speaking of those in Christ that are in relationship with Him yet still want to give up. Why don't we pay attention to our spouses and love them through that season of change?

It could be a great opportunity for the relationship, as change is not always a bad thing, it could be simply the way we handle that change. As you think about it, is it really change, or could it be renewing, refreshing or a necessary rejuvenation even?

Have you ever noticed how styles repeat themselves over time? Not so much for the fragrances or scent, they may be similar, but I cannot say the very scent or fragrance repeats. So, in that aspect, there is change. It would also be fair to say they are just enhanced in some way, but they are often very similar to the old but to us it's new. We may not throw them away, but we certainly allow them to rest.

This plays out in many areas of our lives, but the season may be different for everyone because change is necessary as we grow. Often what we think needs to be changed is simply a need for refreshment or rest of what is already there. Desires can completely change and that is okay. But think about it, that person you thought you just needed to have in high school or college is no longer as desirable today as they were back then. Some of you even feel sick to the stomach when you think back to why you desire them in the first place. It wasn't them; it was you.

We change over time, as do our desires, likes, wants and expectations. As a child you could not pay me to eat Brussel sprouts, the mere thought of them would make me want to puke. Some of us feel the same about an ex or two, they make you want to puke when you think about ever desiring them. Or someone you looked at back then in pure disgust, now you're probably head over heels in love with them today. Same with me with Brussel sprouts, I desire Brussel sprouts now, more than I do pizza at times, something I really love. Did the Brussel sprouts change?

Nope, I did.

What about looking back at pictures that you may have taken a few years back wondering why the heck anyone would allow you to be seen alive in either the hair style or cut and possibly the outfit you were wearing. Those clothing etc. didn't change, your taste, desires and wants changed. Same applies in marriage in the bedroom.

After about two years or so of living in the same house, having the same mundane schedule, and several times of making love. You can almost predict what the next move is of your partner especially if they remember that move is what gets you excited wanting to please you. Often, if they are becoming discontented and have come to a point of just self-pleasing, they may be in a place of performing a move that makes you wish it would hurry up and be over.

So, let's break that down.

I can speak from a woman's perspective, if I am wooing and hollering when my husband does something during a love making session, again, that gets him excited seeking and feeling my excitement rise. Naturally, he is going to want to continue to make this particular move. However, if I have become bored yet still, I am giving my husband the same reactions cheering him on in a sense, what will his response be? You've guessed it. And he is going to get up feeling like he is the man and you're rolling your eyes hoping he hurry up and leave so you can truly release on your own what you just pretended he had done just a moment ago.

In either case, there is a lack of positive communication. I say positive communication because even negative communication is communication. Therefore, depending on the situation, there may be deeper issues than those of which are in the bedroom and could require serious fasting and possibly counseling. It's important to effectively communicate with your spouse about what works for you now. That does not mean you say something like "You're not pleasing me anymore," or "This is getting old." Instead, you could say "Baby, I'd love it if you touch me here or kiss me here." Or plan a romantic night to implement some new things that may help increase the mood. But it is important to know your partner well. The last thing you want to do is offend each other.

The Bible says the marriage bed is undefiled but that does not mean you should pull out a whip and start striking your mate. Some may like this, but others may be offended. So positive communication is imperative for a healthy marriage and sex life.

Imagine this: what if your spouse had been sexually assaulted and you were unaware, role playing aggressively may not be ideal. Nor would a role of the "other woman." Your spouse could possibly be triggered if they were cheated on previously. So, it's important to know what your partner's triggers are at this stage. As there may have been some things that have happened prior to the marriage you are not fully aware that it could play a role in present sexual desires. Knowing and understanding where you both are today is vital. As is your love life, so have those open discussions, maybe over a relaxing night in, romantic night out or even through a game. I wouldn't encourage this conversation during your love making session. Instead, do it ahead of time or right after, it all depends on your person. If possible, in a setting that will allow you to maybe begin to explore those possibilities.

A good friend shared from previous experience with her husband, she wanted to implement something new, and she did so during her intimate time with her husband. However, again you must know your mate and know when or how to bring up certain situations. She apparently didn't at the time, and he became quite offended to say the least and hinted around to the idea that she had been cheating. She then became offended and unfortunately the entire mood was lost. When she tried to revisit the conversation later, he was then in a place of coming out directly by asking "Are you cheating? Who have you tried that with to know if you like it?"

She says she knows today that he was not very mature in his place in the marriage nor was she because she immediately jumped to the defense wondering if he was asking because he had been cheating. Needless to say, that ended but it was not due to that conversation, instead the lack of others that were very necessary but unfortunately not able to be had due to the lack of emotional maturity on both their parts. So again, know your spouse.

What I believe many of us fail to realize is we are two individuals coming together as one in God's eyes. That means all of our experiences, differences, challenges etc. can often clash with one another. If both are not secure in who they are as individuals or lack emotional maturity/intellect, it could be a breeding ground for trouble. Not just in the bedroom but in the marriage, as a whole. So before even entering into marriage, self-development and identity are key. However, if these things are lacking and marriage has already been established, fasting and possibly counseling/therapy may be necessary.

But for those who are sound in those areas and their biggest struggle is having a desire for something new in the bedroom but don't have a clue how to go about it, I would encourage you to not look for anything new necessarily. Instead, try reinventing what is currently there or once was there but for whatever reason has become stale, dry or less exciting. This again will require positive communication.

I know couples who have known each other for several years as friends before getting married. They thought due to the many years of friendship they had built, they would not have to work as hard in areas of the bedroom as a couple who only knew each other a couple years. That could not be less true. As friends stated, they did not have as detailed conversations concerning their sexual desires or how any phobias might play a part in the bedroom.

For example, one friend stated that though her now husband knew she struggled with claustrophobia, he had no way of knowing being restrained during role play was a huge no for her. She stated that, as adventurous as they both are in the bedroom, he cannot restrain her without triggering that fear or anxiety in her. Same for him, as much as he enjoys TLC around the "two short men in the brown suits," he would refuse her getting to close to his rectum without him wanting to sling her across the room. As they learned later and had been too ashamed to share that there had been sexual trauma of some sort.

Again, this is why counseling, praying and fasting is imperative. Though in both instances, other people may have desired these things, it was not their preference and that's okay. This is why it is important to know each other well because these are two extreme examples, others may be as simple as a woman not wanting her husband to touch her breasts after delivering a baby. She may have enjoyed it before, however the body changes often after childbirth and or nursing your child. This could also be due to the fear of an adverse reaction for the baby such as an increase in possible bacteria or even pain for her. It could be just a season, or it could be permanent. But it must be communicated properly, to avoid disruption in the marriage.

I was in that place once, but I never voiced it, instead I suffered through it to avoid him feeling rejection from me. But my lack of communication disrupted my desire for my husband. This led to me not be able to enjoy our times of intimacy as I normally would be and in return this caused him to second guess his ability to please me. I would be encouraging saying "It's not you," but I didn't go into detail about what it really was as I did not want to turn him off. Only it did just that as my silence left the only other possibility for him, it was him.

I know there are other factors that play a part in the bedroom that cause friction, discomfort, or decreased desire. That is natural but this is where the right communication comes in. Don't be afraid to speak your desires unlike I was, because it could cause a domino effect. I have heard women say they had gotten to a point were making love to their husband was more of a chore, instead a pleasure. This could be hormonal for some, but in these cases, it was lack of proper communication. Even in those cases of hormonal changes, I strongly believe that proper communication could help as well as diet, change of lifestyle, therapy etc., in most cases.

Do you remember the movie, Green Mile? The husband could not sexually please his wife because of a condition he had. Something as simple as urinating was a challenge for him and extremely painful. His wife understood, but I'm sure that didn't help her frustration. However, because of her love for him and her heart to understand, she didn't stress him nor go out to cheat. This was something he could not help; however, I do believe he could have aided her in that area in helping her release even if he couldn't.

Again, the marriage bedroom is undefiled. To his credit, when he was able to get miraculous healing, he made up for lost times. Not everyone has the same results but for those who are struggling with health issues, it's a good place to pray for your marriage. Tune in to what it is God is needing from you or your marriage. I'm not a health expert but there is nothing like eating a clean diet, exercise, meditation and getting plenty of rest to aid in your sexual stimuli. I believe when you have great healthy communication in and out of the bedroom with your partner and a healthy lifestyle, there are no limitations on where that relationship can go.

I know many married couples that also believe it and apply it in their marriage. They've learned that what they eat, drink and or entertain can have an adverse effect on their marriage. I'm told that before they eat, they are not just thinking about their own body, but union. The word says marriage makes you one with your spouse. They understand the importance of agreement; how can a healthy marriage stand without agreement? I say 'healthy' because there are some unhealthy marriages that last for years. I know couples who hate each other but will never leave, instead they bring others into the marriage.

I even met a gentleman that in a roundabout way, made light of the fact he and his wife do not have time for each other, nor does he sleep well at night much less love making. He stated he and his wife do workout, but it is always separate from one another. It was disheartening to hear they were pretty much in a dreadful marriage. I suggested in a gentle way how to rekindle the flames in the marriage, making each other a priority. I suggested that love making could help tackle two of his problems, lack of sleep as well as quality time together, while still getting plenty of exercise.

The key in life is to allow ourselves to embrace different seasons but not allow that season to break us. Look at the world around us. As the season changes, so does the world around us. We must change what we wear for the weather in most areas. Birds fly south when it begins to get cold. The trees and grass may wither, the flowers fade. There can often be droughts in the rivers and creeks around us at times. But like the God we serve, it is never without purpose. Once that season is over, trees blossom again as well as flowers. The creeks and rivers fill and begin their normal flow. So, though situations may seem dead in our lives, there still may be a lot of life still there, we simply need to adjust to that change of season, be it physically, emotionally or mentally.

We must be flexible in any sort of season of change, respecting the change in others adjusting accordingly to that change. I am one that has a hard time with change, as I better understand season, instead of rejecting, becoming angry or frustrated, I now ask myself when seasons change in my life, how can I adjust to this change of season? What can I learn from it and how can this season be beneficial to me moving forward?

Grant it, changes aren't always easy, but who never said it would be? Also, if we stand in the word of God for our guide, we will never go wrong. For the word says though the grass may wither, flowers fade, but the word of God will last forever. That means we can stand sure footed in the word of God and place our marriage in His hands and it too can last forever. Not by force, but by grace, love, patience and all of the fruit of the spirit.

Okay, you have reached that point of this chapter where you have an opportunity to share about your season of change. Can you relate to this experience?

Please take a moment to reflect on those times and take that space below to share your own experience in a season of change.

____

____

MY SON SUFFERED

Once my son was born and after enduring and overcoming so much, I was truly looking forward to and overly excited to bring my baby boy into this world. After losing his dad, I was alone most of my pregnancy, being in a different state from friends and family.

I was relieved and grateful when my sister-friend finally got in touch with me. She and I had not spoken for years due to life happening. But something, I believe it to be the Holy Spirit had her reach me by WhatsApp. She immediately went into action helping me in many different areas.

She and her husband, my Joely (he hates that name) were there by my side throughout the last few months of my pregnancy and during delivery. Like my previous two deliveries there was pain and fear but there became calm, and I was able to rest. I was enjoying rest so much I didn't know I was in labor, I thought it was simply back pain. My sister-friend demanded that I go to the hospital right away.

Once there, they admitted me immediately to prepare me for delivery. I was already six centimeters dilated. That means my uterus had almost opened enough for me to push. Hours later, there was no movement, and baby boy decided he wanted to stay a little longer. Both my sister-friend and I walked and laughed, eventually falling asleep because we were at a standstill.

In the early hours of the morning, I remember being wakened by pressure I could not explain. No pain, just pressure. My best friend took a look and there was a head. Right away she called for doctors, but baby boy was not waiting for the doctor, not the nurse staff, not anyone, he was ready to come now. Thankfully a nurse caught him right in time.

Isn't that like God?

We get a glimpse of a blessing and because of the struggles up to that point, we want it now. Only God often makes us wait. We can do whatever our little hearts may want but it's not until we rest in him, not stress in trust, then it comes in suddenly. What we may have been praying for finally comes. Only what we may have asked for may come with its own struggles, struggles we could have never imagined would come with such a blessing.

As much as I prayed for my son, I was not prepared for what came with him. I remember the nurse saying, "OH MY GOD!" Not because of how quickly he shot out, but how he looked once he finally came out. My son had extremely strong features of down syndrome. They let me hold him for a brief second and I remember crying slightly from embarrassment and regret. We all knew there was a strong chance of Downs but not to this extent.

How could this be?

I prayed, and I had faith that he would not reflect anything that the tests and doctors had indicated. Yet instead, my prayers were not answered, God had indeed rejected them. I was heartbroken, saddened.

"My girls had been perfect, how is it that my son was so imperfect? Why would God give me this child with no help from a father," I thought. The world will judge him, he will be picked on, he will stand out in society, he will not be accepted. Negative thoughts ran through my head. I cried as I looked down at this little Japanese looking baby.

The Holy Spirit touched me and reminded me that all this baby needed was love. He reminded me of everything I feared for my new baby boy, are all the things that I have personally experienced in my life. Not because of how I may have looked, but because of what God has put on the inside of me. The same rejection that Christ experienced as well as others who follow Christ.

Instantly, I felt a level of love for this beautiful gift of life in a boy child. How often do we take time to be thankful for what has come when it doesn't rightly look like what we think it should look like? I had been praying for my son, God gave him to me, so who am I to complain or be in discontent for the type of child he decided for me to have?

God chose me to be this baby's mom as He knew he would receive the special love and care he needed because I personally knew what it was like not to have it. That regret and the moment of embarrassment now became an unconditional love like I never knew I could give. That kind of love that I now understand God to have for us as His children. It doesn't matter what we look like or who we belong to on this earth; His love is everlasting and unconditional. I kissed my son telling him I love him no matter what and that I would protect him. I didn't realize I would soon have to put those words into play sooner than later.

They took my son to finish cleaning him and to check his weight, length, etc. They were taking longer than I thought they should to examine my child. I asked for my son back so I could nurse him and continue bonding. They stated the doctors were working on him and he would be in my arms shortly. In that very moment, I began to feel faint and began to shiver. I was losing a lot of blood, but they were not yet aware, nor was I. I remember when they finally brought my baby back to me, I couldn't even hold him. I don't remember what happened after that. I do remember praying, asking God please don't take me because I needed to be here to protect my son.

I was freezing at this point; I can't tell you what the doctors were doing to help but I needed warmth due to the amount of blood I was losing. The Holy Spirit whispered to me hot tea. I somehow mumbled this to my sister-friend, "I need hot tea."

She immediately jumped up to get it. By this time there was concern I'd need a blood transfusion. But God had other plans. I begged God not to allow this. I received the hot tea and immediately felt better. No, it wasn't the tea that caused me to no longer need the transfusion, instead it was my obedience of simply getting tea and trusting more in my prayers and not the present situation. This was a key moment as I truly began to doubt if God was hearing me earlier on, I believe this was confirmation that He had.

I was able to hold my son and was taken to the mommy and baby unit. The day was going well, though there were some obvious issues with baby boy, there was nothing out of the norm and nothing that raised concern. The baby went to have normal infant testing which gave me time to rest and allowed my sister-friend to go rest as well.

For some reason, fear set in and I began crying when I thought about everything I needed to do. I called one of my good friends at the time who was so encouraging. He stated to me, not knowing what the prophet told me early on in my pregnancy, "This boy is your gift, this child is going to make things better for you. Your tears of sorrow will soon turn into tears of joy, do not fear."

Then another friend at the time said to me, "Why are you worrying? You know who you serve, God's got this, so pull yourself together."

These two statements were what I needed. Time went by and I was able to shower and freshen up. Shortly after, my sister-friend came in with my favorite lamb dish, I ate it and was happy. My tummy was full, but it had been some time since my son left for his hearing test.

I grew concerned.

I asked the nurse where my son was and she is replied, "They are almost done."

I did the only thing I knew to do, I prayed. Then a knock at the door. The person introduced himself as my son's pediatrician. But this visit felt different. He walked in and said to me "Mom, there's good news and there is bad news."

With a calm over me I asked, "Ok what is the bad news?" I always want the bad news first in hopes the good news would cushion the bad.

He spoke. "The doctors are going to come in here and tell you all kinds of things about your son."

I said, "Okay, what's the good news?"

He said, "There is NOTHING wrong with your son," and he left.

I never saw him again, and no one knew who he was because he was not a pediatrician but instead sent from God. No one knew who this "pediatrician" was, I never saw him again. He was a prophet or an angel that presented himself as my son's pediatrician. So, I believed what he said; he was a messenger from my Heavenly Father.

I was at peace, yet I still was not emotionally prepared for what would come from my next visit. Before this, I made myself busy and began to bathe my little daughter. In the middle of her shower, a doctor came in, she did not knock on the bathroom door, just simply allowed herself in. I could see in her face something was wrong. I asked, in a trembling voice, "Where is my son?"

Not answering, she just asked if I had someone to get my daughter while helping me shower her. I asked again as tears began to fall, "Where is my child?" Very gently told me she would take me to him but wanted me to know the doctors are working hard. I knew something was wrong, so I began to cry. I trusted God yet I said, "What is wrong with my son?"

Again, very gently she stated, "He is in the NICU." I cried harder because she went on to say that he isn't breathing well and needs assistance. I felt like time stood still because I just could not believe all that had already happened during the pregnancy, and now I am dealing with this.

I felt like I was going to faint. In that moment, the Lord whispered to me, "I have prepared you for a time such as this, trust me."

Well, at this point that's all I had. I had no more strength, and the only strength I could rely on came from the Lord. I cried out to Him, help me my Lord as we walked through what seemed like mile long hallways. I kept saying, I trust you, Lord. When my daughter and I reached my almost lifeless son lying in this incubator, I could see all these tubes going through him. My baby was laying there looking lifeless.

I almost lost it, "This cannot be so," I cried out. I screamed, "WHAT HAPPENED? He was FINE when he left me!"

But I remembered that it was this moment that I needed to remind God of what He said, not what I see or my pain. Plus, I had to be an example for my 6-year-old who was standing there with me watching her baby brother's pale body in this machine.

Another doctor walked up, as did a nurse, and began to tell me Jeremiah needed surgery on his heart, a feeding tube and something to help his lungs as they were not fully developed. I rebuked it! I knew who I served. I believed what was prophesied over me and my child. I proclaimed, "It is well," in my spirit.

I mustered up the strength to speak as the tears rolled down my eyes and I told the doctor, "With all due respect doctor, the Bible says let every man be a LIAR and God be the truth, so I rebuke that statement which is spoken over my son."

She continued to speak, acknowledging my faith but standing firm on her science. I went into prayer, placing my hands on my tiny little baby boy inside of the incubation unit and I cried out to the Lord. The more she spoke the harder I prayed, ignoring any report from the devil, believing only what the Holy Spirit said.

I remember hearing the nurse interrupt the doctor as she tried to interrupt my prayer, "Don't you see her praying?"

At that moment, a calm came over me. I dried my eyes, smiled at my daughter and my son and said with confidence, "He will be okay."

My daughter and I went back to our room to prepare for her to be picked up as I knew I would be there for some days. I still had my mommy unit but spent most of my time in the NICU with my son praying over him, kissing, and adoring his very being. Unfortunately, I did not rest, I did not want to miss a moment with him, so I refused to sleep.

My faith was strong, but my body was tired, still a little stressed and sad. So, my faith was not as strong as it needed to be otherwise, I would be able to rest. But I didn't, this caused the delay in my milk. Preventing me from the ability to feed Jeremiah. I was so emotional as he was losing weight. They suggested I go home to rest; I refused.

I came in with my son; I will leave with him. But unfortunately, they had no space for me to stay in the NICU, and I was almost forced to go home. But I prayed, shortly after I was informed by a very kind nurse that they were able to make some adjustments which would allow me to stay in the NICU with Jeremiah.

While in the NICU, I proceeded to feed my son but there was no milk yet of course, but my body wouldn't even produce the pre-milk called colostrum. This was a concern because breastfeeding has always been a must for me with my children. If any of my children needed it, it was Jeremiah.

My baby was hungry and growing weaker by the minute. The doctors suggested the lab produced milk which is fine for those that cannot produce it. However, I knew and trusted that eventually I would produce my own nourishment for my baby, the one God Himself had given me. Only I was being disobedient and didn't realize how that disobedience would cause my son to suffer more.

The Bible says obedience is greater than sacrifice. In this case, I did not understand that. I was willing to sacrifice my son's life and mine out of ignorance instead of being obedient and simply resting. God needed me to trust Him, instead I was trusting him to a degree and trusting me more.

Sadly, my son was losing ounces. This may not seem like much, but when you are only a few lbs., every ounce counts. I continued to try to latch him but to no avail. A nurse suggested pumping, only drops at a time would come. Yet we were hopeful it would suffice, and we fed him through a syringe because it was not enough to even put into a bottle. This was not pleasing to doctors as his weight loss increased. The doctors suggested a feeding tube, I refused.

After another day, he was losing so much weight, they began to go to the board to vote against me for the sake of Jeremiah. But I knew I needed to protect my son as I told him I would when he was born. I was not giving him man-made milk (nothing against mothers who do) but I believed God when He said He had prepared me for such a time as this. He has allowed me as Jeremiah's mother to be equipped with all the nutrients his body needed at the time. I simply needed rest to produce it, but I was not going home.

Thankfully, a worker came in asking if I would mind another mother's milk if she could get it for him. Though she explained it wouldn't be likely as it was from the milk bank and only for babies that were born premature were entitled to breast milk. Jeremiah was born over 8 lbs.; it was unlikely he would qualify due to his healthy weight. But Glory be to God, it was approved. Jeremiah was being fed, and I could try to pump my milk. They even assigned a nurse to care for Jeremiah, so I could rest during the night. My only job was to rest. I was too stubborn to do it on my own, so Holy Spirit spoke through the medical staff. Because of their obedience, I was able to rest. This allowed my milk to come in full force. Jeremiah had put on a few ounces, and I was able to hold him. The milk was coming, which was great but unfortunately it did not last, and Jeremiah was not properly latching on. Jeremiah needed to latch on to my breast so his saliva could communicate what his body was lacking, and my body would produce it.

Finding a bottle for him was another challenge. Thankfully, he was still gaining a little weight as well as resting. So was I, I was also eating and resting. Everything was finally lighting up so much. I was no longer worried about Jeremiah. Instead, my attention turned to the other babies in the NICU. I found myself praying for them and crying out to God for their family. I even asked if I could go care for them while Jeremiah was asleep. I just could not take hearing those babies cry, and no one was there to comfort them.

I cried out to God for them each night. The more I prayed for them, the more Jeremiah became stronger. My hungry baby began to latch on immediately to get his portion of his mommy's milk. I was overjoyed by the movement of my faith in God. I knew it had only been my faith that God could do it.

No matter what we face, if we simply believe, we may receive. In that moment, I looked down at my nursing baby, I could literally see my son's neck transforming to what many would say is "normal." When he was born, his neck was very wide for his little body. The Lord showed me because of my faith, this child was transforming right before my eyes. I was so honored to see the hand of the Lord continue to move in my life and my faith continued to develop. We left the hospital after only days of being in NICU. What was said to be possibly months, was only one week. I gave God all praises.

But it was not over. Not one bit.

Time went by, several complications, possibilities of surgery, late nights, yet trusting and believing. Jeremiah continued to have slight breathing issues. We were in and out of the hospitals but each time, there ended up being nothing wrong with Jeremiah. Each overnight or weekly stay in the hospital for Jeremiah became opportunities for me to pray for the other children there. God had a great purpose, and he was using what was said to be an issue for Jeremiah, to be a blessing for others.

However, even when it's purposeful, it's not always easy. I remember crying out to God, after several sleepless night. "Why does my son continue suffering for other people?"

I was angry and just wanted answers. Like He did when I first encountered the Holy Spirit, He answered. "MY Son Suffered. What makes you think yours would not have to?"

Immediately, I cried in forgiveness. I remembered what Christ endured for us, repented and cried in thanks of the great sacrifice.

Jeremiah continued to suffer and though I continued to cry, I knew it was with purpose. I felt like Mary must have felt when her Son was going through His suffering. But we both trusted God and knew it was for a greater good.

I still cried when Jeremiah had his episodes, but I would rejoice and praise because I knew one day it would be over, I just didn't know when. Today, no surgeries and no longer any breathing issues, my son is healed. I hadn't realized exactly when it happened, but suddenly, I remembered Jeremiah was sleeping so peacefully through the night, no longer struggling to breathe, no interruption in his breathing. God had done what He promised! Weeping endured for the night, but joy indeed came in the morning.

Hey there, what are your thoughts after reading this chapter? Take a moment and think on an experience you had where you had to remember how having a mustard seed of faith can make even the impossible, possible; did it make you feel grateful for the great sacrifice of the suffering of Christ?

Please take a moment to reflect on those times and use space below to share your own experience.

____

____

____

____

____

____

____

MEL SPEARS

Chapter 11

BE THE HOLY, not HOLEY

One midafternoon, my 9-year-old at the time says to me out of the blue, "Mommy, I can see your panties, then she giggled.

"I said no you cannot, do not tell stories, God does not like that."

I was confident that my panties were not showing as I do not wear revealing clothes. It's never been my thing, especially around my children. Besides, at that point, I had been out driving since early morning, in and out of the car. I just knew had I been exposed, someone would have noticed and said something. She must be mistaken or playing one of her little pranks.

My little one was famous for pranking mommy. Only this time my baby was not playing nor was she pranking me. I knew this because she said it again. My baby said, "I can really see your panties mommy," and she giggled, yet I knew she was serious. At this point I was concerned again; I had been gone all day. So, I wondered if my panties were showing, how many others have seen it and not told me? Just how much of myself have I exposed to the world and how much I am now exposing to my little daughter?

Rushing over to the mirror, I looked frantically, praying there was some mix-up. Only there was no mix up. My baby was right; my panties were indeed exposed. Thankfully, it was not as obvious as I was thinking. The only way anyone would be able to see the exposure would be if they were close on me or in the light. I wondered why didn't I notice this before putting on my pants?

I remember I had gotten dressed in the dark. I wanted to avoid waking the rest of the house as I left extremely early. I laughed it off with my daughter because I could now see what her little eyes could see, she was the light. Now aware of how my pants were thinning, I still did not see the need to change as it wasn't "that" bad. I wasn't going anywhere, and it wasn't too obvious, besides only my little daughter was here with me for now.

As I sat on the chair, preparing to do some work from home, I looked down at my pants. I noticed there was a hole. "Where did this come from?" I thought.

As I examined further, holes were everywhere in my pants. In that moment, I heard the Holy Spirit whispering how the thinning in my pants and the deeper look finding holes, reflected my walk at the time in God. In the process of trying to be holy, holes were found all through me. I was not yet *whole*. Just like I dressed in the dark to avoid waking others, my still walking in the darkness was hindering the awakening of others.

This revelation was crazy to me, it wasn't anything about my pants, instead, my soul. I had work to do. I began weeping for clarity because I did not understand. I was doing the best I could. I was saved, sanctified and filled with the Holy Ghost. What more could I do? I wondered how it was possible that I still had so many holes so to speak and not quite as Holy as I thought?

I was confused and wanted to understand better. It took months for that revelation to come. There were still issues I had not yet addressed. Those I had not surrendered fully to God; I was in pain, and I was hiding it in the dark. Yet when we walk fully in the light, God will allow those things to be exposed so they can no longer have the hold over us as they had before.

It's like still desiring to walk in the dark instead of fully in the light. As excited as I was and still am in my walk, I must stay close to the word so I can be cleansed from my past. Being cleansed from the past eliminates the need to "get dressed in the dark."

Unlike those others that did not see the holes in my pants, there are many in the world just like me, they too are in darkness, so they may not see my holes. It took the pureness in my little 9-year-old to boldly share I was "exposed." Though she had no idea, it was more about my soul, she was the beginning of the need to look deeper.

God used my princess to help in the beginning of my healing. I had suppressed so much from my childhood that I had been strong all my life. Being in Christ, I believed all was well. What I didn't realize is I was bleeding on others unintentionally; I was still in bondage from my past and crying in the dark pretending all was well. But God seen it all and it was time to heal these holes in my soul so the fullness of my walk in Christ could come full circle. Often, we can't see it in ourselves, but God will put some little eyes on you that are pure and full of light that will make you check and examine yourself.

Like me, many of us could be in denial of what God is trying to show us due to ignorance. But if we are open and have the desire to learn. The Holy Spirit will so gently show us. I can go as far as saying, He will show us either way, it's up to us to believe and desire change. The continued breakdown of this revelation pierced me so deeply. I went deeper allowing the Holy Spirit to wrap His love around me. When we recognize the love of God, we will embrace any necessary change He shows us for our journey ahead. There is nothing that He does to harm us, instead it is to prosper us.

Once again, you have reached a point in another chapter where you can reflect on any experience that relates to my struggle in recognizing brokenness within. Take a moment, pause and reflect on your own experiences in this area, find a scripture that you may use in times like this.

Chapter 12

A PURSUIT TO HAPPINESS

I thought happiness was something people like me gave to others; the happiness I'd received would pull directly from their happiness as it was my job to be pleasing to people, at least I thought!

For years happiness was chasing me, I say chasing me as clearly, I was running from it. I was not aware of what happiness was at that time. Although it came, I would not receive it. Not genuine happiness, the kind not based on what I did or received from others, that true inner happiness, a particular peace, joy even. This type of happiness was not tangible, it's something no one could give, nor could anyone take it away. This sort of happiness was uncomfortable for me as it required something from me that I was not quite mature enough to face at the time. I was not ready to face *Me*.

You know that self-reflection.

Therefore, pleasing others came easy as it allowed me to focus on the needs of others instead of focusing on my own needs. I stayed busy, no stopping for me. Any hint or the feeling of a rise of what may have needed to be addressed in me, hurts, pains, fears etc., I was out of there.

I was a big-time runner and was good at it, or so I thought. What I learned the hard way is that I cannot run from myself, and I surely cannot run from God. At the end of it all, me, God and I are always there. So, I learned a different method of coping with my issues. I had mastered the skill of acknowledging the pain, hurt and fears but I was still not ready to fully address them.

I began covering the wounds with whatever type of band-aid I could find. I figured with the bandages, no one would see my hurts. I would not look weak to them, nor would they be able to take advantage of me in ways I had seen other women be taken advantage of. I had nursed these wounds as best as I could, but unfortunately, nursing a thing does not always mean it is healed. I can truly say I was not healed at all, and those wounds began to bleed on others and in many ways became infected. I was fixing everyone else's problem, running to the aid of anyone in need but when it came down to me, I was not as attentive.

I lacked self-love and this is why I did not have inner happiness, nor did I genuinely have that peace I needed to be free from the bondage of my past. I had not quite matured in a manner of self-love. Unhappiness and misery required so much from me, but I was used to giving and people needing so much from me without having to replenish me. I became comfortable there, then it caused me to in a sense, resist or resent happiness because it required so much for me. I didn't quite understand until I reviewed the notion of Love your neighbor as you love yourself. I did not know how to love me, so how could I possibly love anyone else?

This was the start of my happiness.

Holy Spirit took me back to the age of 21 where I would become so angry and determined to show others, I was not a victim. Up until that point, I had been a Martha, you know the busy body in the Bible? She was so busy working for everyone but for Jesus that he had to call her name twice. I became used and abused from babysitting, cooking, cleaning, ironing etc. I thought I enjoyed these activities, instead I knew I needed to keep my stay. My siblings and I hopped around for years from house to house, never having a home. I became burned out and I had to create my own mental place of safety.

This took me to a place of darkness, lashing out at people and being a know it all. Because I was twenty-one, I had my own place and my own car earning my own money. I thought I was cute and had it going on. But underneath, I was broken, a little girl crying out. My cries were silenced because no one would hear them anyway, so what's the use?

A protective wall was created, and I was safe, yet I didn't cry. I lacked emotions because I was determined not to be seen as the weak little girl who I truly was, and I wore a mask for years. I recall my mother having surgery on her brain to have an aneurism clamped. I was so afraid, I cried.

When my mom awoke hours later, she spoke of my sister crying so hard before her surgery and comforting her. I exclaimed, "No that was *me* mommy."

She said to me as she laughed "That was your sister, you don't cry."

I pleaded that it was me and that my sister was not there. She ignored me because in her mind, she could not fathom the idea of me expressing any emotions so it could *not* be me. It wasn't until after having children that I began to express myself more or showed emotions, but there were still limits.

One day after receiving Christ, I remember crying for hours, nonstop, it was if someone unclogged a faucet of backed up tears because they did not stop. Now I am a crybaby, I cry about everything, the funniest part of that is people talk about me being a crybaby now, showing too much emotion and taking on the hurts and pains of others. I was confused; if I don't show emotions, I'm mean and if I show emotions, I'm too sensitive. Thankfully, during this journey the Holy Spirit allowed me to see that I needed balance and that balance only came from a strong relationship with Christ Jesus. I was able to better understand to love anyone else, I first had to learn to love me and the only way to love me was to love the one who truly loved me. There is no satisfaction in pleasing people or even self, that the greatest satisfaction only comes from surrendering my life to Christ.

I began to say 'NO' to others and 'YES' to God. Because the Martha Spirit was still lingering in me, I was a people pleaser. I was known for being the doer, even if not asked, I would leap to volunteer to do whatever was needed at that time.

I remember a relationship I was in when the daughter of the man was given a birthday party. Being who I am, I was the only one running around. At the time it didn't bother me but as I reflect on that moment, everyone else, both her parents and grandparents in attendance, were sitting back laughing and enjoying themselves. Here I was being a Martha.

Like other times, as soon as what I did for them or didn't do for someone did not please them or they were ungrateful, I would be become bitter, angry, or mad. But the problem wasn't them, it was me. I did not at the time know how to cast my cares upon Jesus as He so kindly requested throughout the Bible. I wanted to take it on myself because of course I could do it better than Jesus, right? WRONG!

The more I did, the more stressed I became. I was angry. Again, it was *me*, not them. They did not know how to appreciate or love me because like me, they too were broken, unhappy and unbalanced. So, unlike what I thought, the more I gave the more they took and the less they would feel required to give. I became depleted and empty, still trying to pour from an empty cup into bottomless containers.

On many occasions, people that were close to me would tell me to sit down, relax but that was not my norm. Since I was a child, I had been a doer for everyone else. I recall several other instances, however the last and final one was one Christmas. I said I would not cook but I did. I said I wouldn't do all the work, but I did.

I recall going to my room so exhausted as not one person helped except for my love at the time. We were both drained, but he knew how to say no, it was me who did not. I recall him asking, "What's wrong?"

The Holy Spirit was dealing with me, because once again, I was so busy being a Martha, I couldn't hear him clearly. He made it so I would not be happy in my spirit, and I didn't want to do anything nor watch anything. There were other things associated with that as well that I will go into later in the book.

Back to the story… I could only pray, I had to stop and pray so I could hear God clearly, to be set free. That girl that once was happy, long as others were happy, was no more. The mask I was forced to wear for so long was peeled back. It still took time to allow the residue to be removed. But one day I cried out to Jesus, help me please, I am broken I am unhappy, and I am bitter. Glory be to God he allowed my 'NO' to others to be gentle but affirmed, not angry but grounded in that NO. He then gave me **Matthew 6:33**, although I didn't quite understand it at first, I'm a bit slow at times. Thankfully, Jesus is patient with helping me to understand. The words of that scripture rang in my spirit, "Seek first the kingdom of God and His righteous and all these things will be added to you."

WAIT, you mean to tell me all I need to do is go to my daddy who is LOVE, all knowing, merciful, forgiving etc. and learn of his Son's ways and He will do the rest, adding **ALL** these things to me. Folks, once I got that revelation, it became extremely clear to me. I had it backwards, I was seeking after man, literally and all I had to do is seek the King of all Kings he would add the All.

That's exactly what He did. The more I sought after Kingdom ways the more righteous I desired to become. I still didn't get everything correct but that's not what it said. It says "seek," so because I have a heart to do so, it's all being added. So, this is where I have found joy and peace. A happiness that I nor man has given me but that of which I have received from our Heavenly Father.

No matter the season I may be in, the more I focus on the 'Kingdom way,' and get out of *my* way the more blessings that come my way. One person had been here for years but as I started this chapter, I realized I had been running from Him as he represented happiness. However, he continued to chase me. This is because he understood.

He never wavered as he knew what God had promised him. More about this later in the book…….

In this season, I've learned to spend less time trying to fix everyone else's problems or running to their aid, which gave me more time to fix myself and God knows I still need work. But too often we leave our own homes to fix someone else's, and the devil leaves their home, then shows up at ours, yet our home is not covered properly.

I truly understand the scripture about taking the beam out of your own eye first so we can see clearly to help our brother take the speck out of his. No that's not what it says verbatim, but you get the gist of it. Now I encourage you to go to **Matthew 7**, read it, and study it so you get the full picture of what it is saying. I pray the Holy Spirit will bless you with understanding.

Here we go! Time to self-reflect!

Take a moment and think of an experience where you may have realized your lack of happiness, joy or even peace. Please take a moment to reflect on those times and use space below to share your own experience.

____

____

____

____

____

____

____

____

MEL SPEARS

Chapter 13

THE BATTLE IS NOT MINE

As you read in the previous chapter, I had been delivered from what I call the *"Martha spirit."* It was a place of striving, overdoing, and over-carrying, well-intentioned service that had quietly slipped into self-reliance. Though the deliverance was real, the residue of that spirit lingered longer than I expected. What I did not yet understand was that deliverance does not always mean instant maturity. Sometimes freedom is immediate, but wisdom is progressive.

God, in His infinite mercy and strategy, had already begun to teach me through the very environment He had placed me in. My car, what

I affectionately call my *"ministry on wheels"* became a sacred space. It was more than transportation; it was a moving altar. God was intentional about the individuals He placed in my vehicle. Often, I did not need to say much. Sometimes my testimony spoke. Other times, silence allowed the Holy Spirit to do what only He could do. At times, worship music ministered more powerfully than any words I could have spoken. For a season, this ministry flowed with grace. But in the weeks that followed my deliverance, something shifted.

I began to experience a deep emotional and spiritual attachment to several women God had placed in my path. At first, I thought this was compassion Christ-like empathy. But over time, it grew heavier. Their burdens became my burdens. Their pain settled into my spirit as if it belonged to me. I found myself thinking about their struggles long after they were gone, carrying their trauma in my body, sometimes to the point of physical weakness or illness. What I could not yet articulate was that I had crossed a line from intercession into substitution.

A close friend noticed before I did. She observed how drained I was after ministering to these women. It was as if I had given something away that I did not have permission to give. She gently but firmly spoke truth to me: *"It's not healthy for you to leave every encounter feeling this heavy. Their problems are becoming your problems."*

At first, I resisted the idea. After all, wasn't I just loving people the way Christ loved them? Wasn't I available, present, and compassionate? But the Holy Spirit began to reveal a sobering truth: I was not simply caring for people; I was attempting to be their savior.

In a subtle but dangerous way, I had positioned myself as the solution instead of the vessel. Instead of praying and releasing, I was carrying and containing. I was taking on weight that was never mine to bear. In essence, I was trying to do God's job.

That realization humbled me deeply.

Several trusted friends echoed the same concern. They lovingly reminded me that my role was not to fix, heal, or carry but to point, pray, and release. One friend directed me back to a familiar scripture, one I had memorized, taught, and shared countless times: *"Come unto me, all ye that labor and are heavy laden, and I will give you rest"* (**Matthew 11:28**).

It struck me sharply that although I could preach this scripture with conviction, I was not living it. I had invited others to rest in Christ while refusing rest for myself. I had become skilled at teaching surrender while quietly resisting it in my own life.

This was not rebellion; it was simply residue.

Around this same time, I was advised to watch the movie *The Green Mile*. Though it is an older film, its message pierced me in a way I did not expect. The character John Coffey possessed a supernatural gift of healing. But every time he healed someone, he absorbed their sickness, pain, or affliction into his own body. He would physically suffer under the weight of what he took on. His healing was real, but so was the cost.

What struck me most was what happened after the healing. John would open his mouth and release what he had taken in, almost as if he was giving it back to God. In that moment of release, he was free. But when he held onto it too long, it nearly destroyed him.

As I watched, tears filled my eyes.

I saw myself.

I had been healing in the wrong way. I had confused empathy with absorption. I had mistaken compassion for responsibility. I had believed that loving others meant carrying what belonged to them. But I was never called to be a reservoir, I was called to be a conduit. The revelation was unmistakable, my assignment is not to heal, it is to lead people to the Healer.

That truth was both freeing and painful. It required me to let go of an identity I didn't realize I had embraced, the identity of "the strong one," "the helper," "the one who can handle it." It forced me to confront a pride hidden beneath service, the belief that I was needed in a way only God should be needed.

"I am not God."

Saying those words out loud felt like swallowing a hard pill, but it was necessary. Ministry does not require self-destruction. Obedience does not demand exhaustion. Love does not mean self-neglect.

That lingering residue finally lifted when I stopped holding what was never mine to hold.

Before this revelation, I was not whole, even though I thought I was. I was attempting to love others with a love I had not yet fully shown myself. Scripture tells us to *"love your neighbor as yourself,"* not more than yourself, and not instead of yourself. The Bible also says that no one hates their own flesh. I did not hate myself, but I was not kind to myself either.

I overlooked my limits. I ignored my need for rest.

I dismissed my boundaries as selfish.

I spiritualized overextension and called it ministry.

But kindness to self is not selfishness, it is stewardship. Through this process, God taught me something revolutionary, "No" is not a bad word!

I also learned a truth that is simple but profound, I cannot pour from an empty cup! If you do, what you call ministry will eventually become resentment. What you call service will become burnout. What you call love will quietly become obligation.

God never asked me to give what I do not have. He asked me to abide, and from that abiding, allow overflow.

That is the order.

As I look ahead, I am genuinely excited about my next season, not because I will be doing more, but because I will *be* more present. Present with God. Present with myself. Present without pressure. I will no longer give people my core, I will give them the overflow.

For a long time, I wondered, *"Why did this return?"* I thought I had already dealt with it. I thought I had already surrendered this area. But the Lord gently showed me the difference between remorse and repentance.

I had been sorry, but I had not fully turned.

True repentance is not merely feeling bad about behavior; it is allowing God to transform the root. I had repackaged my old patterns and dressed them up as ministry. I had exchanged one form of striving for another. And worse, I had left an empty space where surrender should have been.

Scripture warns us that when a spirit leaves and finds the house empty, it goes and gathers seven more, returning stronger than before. I had removed the behavior but failed to invite the Holy Spirit to fully occupy the space. So, the pattern returned louder, heavier, and more demanding.

But even in that, God's posture toward me never changed.

The solution was the same as it always is: release and refill. I released what was never mine. I repented, not just apologized. I invited the Holy Spirit to fill every space I had tried to manage myself. And once again, I was reminded of the central truth of this chapter:

I do not have to fight for control. I do not have to carry what He already conquered. I do not have to prove my worth through exhaustion. My role is obedience.

His role is outcome. And in that exchange, I finally found rest.

Self-Reflection

Hey there, what are your thoughts after reading this chapter? Take a moment and think on an experience you had where you had to remember how Jesus showed you the battle is not your own.

Please take a moment to reflect on those times and use space below to share your own experience.

____

____

____

____

____

____

____

____

____

____

Chapter 14

DELAYED, NOT DENIED

When it seems like God is doing absolutely nothing, and your life is at a standstill; He is at work on our behalf. He is moving quicker than light on what has already been spoken, which means it has already been done. He simply seeks our obedience for the work to be fulfilled.

An airplane at its achieved height can travel up to 500-600 miles per hour. However, from the window seat on the plane, it looks as if you can walk faster than the plane is going. It seems like you are moving in slow motion.

You plan and wait for the day of travel, board the plane and boom, you know you are going faster than you realize, though it may feel almost at a standstill. So much takes place to get to a particular destination. Whether it is a short or long trip, planning and anticipation takes place. You can plan strategically, crossing every T and dotting every I, yet days feel it will take forever to get there.

Like on a plane, we are given clear instructions on what to do in the event of an emergency landing or if the pressure changes on the plane, your mask will drop down. We are instructed on how to put on a floating device that is located under our seat. They emphasize the importance of putting on your mask prior to assisting anyone else. Like as a first-time flyer, as new followers of Christ we are attentive and tuned in to the Bible as our manual, just like the flight attendant, reading the manual that is attached to the back of the chair in front of us.

After flying several times, we often become so certain that we know what to do. We possibly fall asleep before the demonstration or become distracted by other things like reading a book, listening to an audio, watching a movie or even glancing at them ever so often, wishing they would just hurry up. Sometimes the flight is smooth and sometimes bumpy. At those bumpy moments or during takeoff, seat belts are mandatory among other things. Once you reach a certain level in the air, the seat belt sign may come off which allows you to move about the cabin freely. Though passengers are allowed to leave their seats during the "no seatbelt" period, it's at your own risk or the risk of others so it's not recommended. Landing can be bumpy or smooth as well. Now you have arrived at your destination point. Though you arrive at this place, there is still work to do, whatever that may be; the arrival is simply the beginning.

Isn't the whole 'flight' experience like life at times?

As I got on a plane on a Sunday afternoon after being delayed, the enemy wanted me to feel like it was a denial. I worshiped in the airport while I waited yet another hour before boarding the make-up flight. I'm thinking about how amazing worship was, so wonderful, it touched others in the airport. So much so that one lady greeted me in the lady's room. She was in full gratitude of my response to the "denied access" to my original flight and how my praise in that moment and open fellowship truly touched and encouraged her.

Right next to me, another lady asked if I was the one in the lady's room speaking about what happened to me. She too was encouraged and thought it was so sweet of me to share. In all of this, I reflect on my walk in Christ. Just as the experience of preparing for a flight, flying and landing, my journey is continuous and often unpredictable.

I think about how we grow on this walk, we can get to a point of feeling like we have arrived. We feel like we do not need to read the manual (Bible) as often as we should. I mean we read it several times, or even going into fellowship with others, but may be relaxed in our receiving of what is being said like that of when the flight attendant is speaking. Yet, in instances of turbulence or fear, condemnation may set in our minds. This is when we pray and seek God to help us to get through.

Often when He wants us to sit down, we get up and move ahead of Him. We move ahead of Him because it's like looking out of the window of the slow-moving plane, and we feel like He is not moving. At least not as fast as we want. So, against His instructions of what we should do according to His manual (Bible), some may get discouraged; think He has forgotten about us or He's slow in His response to request. That couldn't be furthest from the truth.

What I've learned in this experience of my delay is God is not a God on *my* time; I instead am on *His*. In all the planning that I make, if it is not according to His purpose, this may deny-*my* plans. *His* plan will go forward. My plan was to miss service but once that door closed, I was able to join after all as well as be a great representation of His Kingdom. I could have been anxious about the door shutting and allowed the "denial" in that moment to change my countenance, but instead I allowed God to get the Glory through me. Did my pressure begin to change? Initially yes, but thankfully He spiritually dropped down a mask, allowing me to breathe. He also allowed me to pull out that floating device in a sense as my legs felt like Jello, as if I would drown. I mean, I sat there for two hours not moving and did not hear the boarding call until last minute; I wanted to lash out. But He allowed me to put on the floating device of Him and no matter how large this issue may seem, it's not greater than my Heavenly Father!

Then I was able to offer kind words to the individuals at the counter. Although they were not kind to me, I responded kindly and told them to have a blessed day. I activated the scripture. One of the scriptures from both services on this day was **Proverbs 3:5-7**, *"Trust in the Lord with all your heart, lean not to your own understanding. Acknowledge Him in all your ways and He will make your path straight."*

That's exactly what happened that day, and I have such joy! I took my focus off the problem and focused on the promise of God to do what I cannot do on my own. As a bonus, I was able to get a much better seat than my original flight next to two wonderful women. Because it was not a full flight, I was able to get a full row to myself. This spoke volumes to me. In my obedience, my plans moved forward in a more comfortable and joyous way, meeting with my soon to be husband God has for me. He is a God of purpose, it says so in **Romas 8:28.** And like this scripture, this situation worked for my good according to His purpose for me.

As I was finishing the writing of this chapter, the flight attendant announced that someone would be getting free 1000-points credit. Already having my tray down, I had not even noticed that on the tray table it stated, "LUCKY SEAT." When I moved from the two wonderful ladies, I was in row 3, but there were two open seats in row 4 behind us. As I moved to that row, I noticed there was row 5 and the entire row was available. I smiled, took that row and wondered why no one else had jumped to it. I remember thinking, this is row 5 which means favor.

You would not believe I then found a nickel on the seat under the chair ahead of me and thought, double favor. And then the announcement, "If you have the yellow "lucky" sticker push the button for the flight attendant," I did just that. In a manner of seconds, I was handed a thousand free points to travel. Some may say it's just luck, but I know that this is the reward in return for my obedience. This is just a small example of the benefits of leaning not to my own understanding! I'm grateful and very much humbled by the move of God in my life.

Hi my friend, what are your thoughts after reading this chapter? Take a moment and think of an experience you had where you had to remember how you may have felt you were denied but realized it was simply delayed?

Please take a moment to reflect on those times and use space below to share your own experience.

____

____

____

____

____

____

____

____

____

BE KIND

As little children, we are taught to be nice. Disciplinary action is the cost of not being nice. Something as simple as telling someone their breath stinks or agreeing that food someone has given us to eat tastes good when it may not. The goal in teaching someone to be nice is to prevent hurting someone's feelings. I recall being told on many occasions, "If you don't have anything nice to say, don't say anything at all." Encouraging many to suppress the truth to avoid hurting feelings.

This type of mindset has taught many of us to become liars as well as a target to be victimized. Being nice may seem to avoid or postpone conflict by softening the truth in an attempt to prevent a negative reaction that may never even happen. It can be rooted in fear, rejection, or even envy, and over time, it can create unhealthy expectations and unhealthy relationships. Although it may appear to be keeping peace, it can actually be ignoring truth. And as we know, it is the truth that sets us free, not a lie used to sugarcoat the circumstance. This is not an encouragement to be rude, not at all. Kindness comes from genuine love and compassion. It is honest, firm, and corrective. Kindness does not simply say what feels good; it says what is for our good. It seeks what is best, not merely what sounds good.

For example, being nice may tell a friend, "You're fine, don't worry about it," even when you can clearly see they are making harmful choices because you do not want to upset them or risk conflict. However, kindness lovingly says, "I care about you too much to stay silent. I think this path is hurting you, and I want better for you." One avoids discomfort to protect feelings in the moment, while the other speaks truth with love to protect the person in the long run.

Think about it, how many times have you come in agreement with something being said, done or asked of you that was not for the benefit for that person, or anyone involved? But because you know what you really thought or stood for may not be perceived as nice, instead you tell them what they want to hear, but not necessarily what would help them; possibly causing hurt to you or others.

So, in all actuality, you lied. Yup, that is the cycle that most Christians fall into. We want please people so bad that we will often say what is opposite of the truth to avoid friction. Rightfully so, because the Bible speaks about being a peace maker. Therefore, the goal is to be 'nice.'

Unfortunately, that's not what the outcome of being 'nice' leads to. Instead, it leads to sin and the misuse of scripture. Something that comes to mind and is often thrown around more than the name of Jesus is, "God knows my heart," or "There's no condemnation for those who are in Christ Jesus." And my favorite, "God is my judge." These all can be found in the Bible in some way shape or form; however, they shamefully are not used in the proper context. Instead, it's misconstruing the text.

It's important that we study the word and understand it, so we don't misunderstand the intent nor continue to throw pieces of the scripture around, making them a cliche instead of a lifestyle. This is when Satan is given access to us. We are new creatures who want to please and be pleased often getting in the way of pleasing the spirit man, then displeasing God. Some may challenge the notion of being nice as it sounds so nice, right? Absolutely it does and in a worldly view it makes lots of sense. Unfortunately, it does not aid in becoming saints or being saints.

As I continue to grow in my relationship with Christ, I learned there is a difference between being 'nice' to one another versus being 'kind' to one another. Jesus was not nice, in fact, there is nowhere in the Bible where we are encouraged to be 'nice.' Don't believe me? Pause right now and find a scripture using the word 'nice.' I'll wait! Find any? If you do, I will truly love for you to contact me as I too am forever learning in this University of Christ. But you won't because the Bible speaks about being 'kind.'

Here are a few reference points from the word to help us understand better. **Colossians 3:12** says, *"Put on then, as God's chosen ones, holy and beloved, compassionate hearts, kindness, humility, meekness, and patience.*

Proverbs 31:26 says, *"She opens her mouth with wisdom, and the teaching of kindness is on her tongue."*

1 Corinthians 13:4-7 says, "Love is patient and kind; love does not

envy or boast; it is not arrogant or rude. It does not insist on its own way; it is not irritable or resentful; it does not rejoice at wrongdoing but rejoices with the truth. Love bears all things, believes all things, hopes all things, endures all things."

1 John 3:18 says, *"Little children, let us not love in word or talk but in deed and in truth."*

Ephesians 4:32 says, *"Be kind and compassionate to one another, forgiving each other, just as in Christ God forgave you."* Do you believe me now?"

Well, it's not me, and this is found through relationships not religion. Religion without true relationships could have us leaning to our own understanding. Nice is not an attribute of Christ, 'kind' however is. Peter was being "nice" to Jesus when Jesus was telling the disciples He must go away and suffer many things. Peter proclaimed to Jesus He must not go. Jesus knew this was not the mind of God, so he rebuked Satan for using Peter because he wanted to be 'nice' to defend Christ. This was the enemy's attempt to hinder the plan God had in place for us all. But because the enemy is sneaky and weak, he made another attempt to use a wicked spirit that will defend Jesus again when they came to take Jesus away. He cut the ear of one of the soldiers. Again, Jesus recognizing the devil at work, He again rebuked Satan telling him to get behind Him. Can you imagine, Jesus pleasing Peter, and feeding into the lie that hides behind nice? It would have meant displeasing God while trying to please man.

Another example that comes to mind is the woman caught in adultery. Jesus could have been nice to her after all the accusers fled. He could have simply said, "God knows your heart," or "There is no condemnation." Or how about my favorite, "God is your judge." awe, that would have been 'nice' of Jesus. I mean she had already been through enough from those evil men. But it would not have been **good** for her.

Jesus instead was kind; He cared more about her soul than He cared about how she felt. He asked her where her accusers were. He didn't even one time condemn her, but no one did. He was 'kind' and told her He would not condemn her, but she was to go and sin no more. It may not have felt as good as 'nice' would have felt but His kindness would work for her good, showing her correction in love.

Had he been 'nice,' she may have fallen back into her sin. Instead, the word says that Mary Magdalena went on to follow Christ. Many would argue that she too was a disciple. So, walking in kindness speaks truth which leads us to a path of righteousness and closer to Christ and our Father God. Being 'nice' instead, speaks lies which leads us to a path of unrighteousness and closer to the world and to the father of lies, the devil.

Moving forward, we all must be intentional with our words when interacting with each other. Many of those things we are taught as children, unfortunately, were not relationship based. Being taught to be "nice" has hindered us as well as those around us. Being 'nice' is not speaking from the word (Bible) but from the world.

As believers, we are no longer of this world, we are simply passing through on a journey to graduate someday with "well done good and faithful servant." We must be soul focused instead of flesh focused. Being doers of the word and not just speakers of it. Dying to our flesh daily as we know in it there is nothing good. If we truly seek God, the spirit can be renewed, and our hearts may be cleaned getting us one step closer to the kingdom.

Just remember, the word says the race is not given to the strong nor the swift but to them who endure forever. This means no matter how tough the test becomes, we must continue fight the good fight until God ultimately calls us home.

Self-Reflection

You are doing great! And once again, it is time to reflect on what you have read. Have you been practicing the spirit of Kindness in your life towards yourself and others? No, judgment either way. Just a great time to think about areas you can improve.

Take a moment, pause and reflect on your own experiences in this area, find a scripture that you may use in times like this.

____

____

____

____

____

____

____

____

____

____

____

____

____

____

____

Chapter 16

IF YOU DON'T LEARN FROM IT, YOU WILL REPEAT IT

When there is a Kingdom assignment on our lives, the enemy too has an assignment against our lives. His assignment is to sabotage **God's** assignment. If we pay close attention, we can beat him at his own game because he is a lazy foe.

Unfortunately, we equip him with the very tools to come after us. He studies us, so he knows our weaknesses, our desires etc. No, he is not God but when we are not focused on the Kingdom and instead focused on our own desires, God allows us to be tested. He doesn't test us but **allows** us to be tested. The word says, He has already created a way out, however, it is up to us to take it. Otherwise, we will find ourselves repeating the same test, entertaining the same spirit in a different body.

"You are my dream girl; you are who I have asked God for all my life."

"So now I can say, dreams do come true!"

BOY BYE!!

That was not my response then of course but keep reading and you will see clearly why this is my response now. 10, 9, 8, 7, 6, 5, 4, 3, 2,1, HAPPY NEW YEAR!!!

I was locked into the arms of the man I thought God had personally hand selected for my life. He was strong, boy was he strong. He was kind and gentle. He was patient and he was willing to put up with my mess.

Lord, know I have some faults. But he looked past them all, allowing me to be open, transparent and free to share my deepest thoughts. He allowed me to be me, a vibrant extrovert, full of life, energy and just passionate about Christ. He was the opposite: an introvert, quiet, reserved and very particular about who he lets in and what he lets out. But he didn't miss a beat when it came to me. He did not play about me; he loved me and was not shy about it.

He was HUGE on PDA. "Public Displays of Affection."

It was amazing, he loved me up. I felt like a teenager again, and I wanted NOTHING. He met EVERY need, mentally, physically, emotionally and financially. It was not an easy win for him though; I had known him for years by the time I finally let him in. We played around with the idea of 'love' very early on, but life happened, and it was just NO! However, he was there, through new loves, heart break and even a baby after my son's father passed suddenly.

He prayed with me, he comforted me, and he waited for me. My heart was guarded; I was sick of losing. He knew it, so he was patient. He helped me dodge the bullet of someone that was after me (same spirit of deception) and he told me he was not good for me. He was so knowledgeable of men who played games.

He was instrumental in giving me the inside scoop on how a man thinks, one of MANY red flags that I ignored early on. He stuck close, being there for the children, and just helping me cope through another possible issue later down the line. Who was this man? He was my angel, or so I thought.

But you've guessed it, this angel broke my heart.

"Are you married or attached to anyone?"

He answered "No, baby."

"Is there anyone who is attached to you?"

He answered, "No baby, I have been single for the past ten years just working and staying busy. I knew deep down you were it for me, if I could not have you, I didn't want anyone. I dated but my heart was with you, you are my dream girl. I let you get away before, but I promised God if I got another chance, I would not mess it up."

I melted, because I too had been praying for God to send my King because who wants to be alone? And hell, if you fall off your bike thirty times, does that mean you don't get back on it again? No, it just means you learn from your mistakes, so you don't fall again, at least not in the same places, right? Whelp, that's what I thought I was doing.

I had strapped on my shoe laces, taken the time to self-reflect. I emptied out all the previous experiences on those past bike rides and y'all I ate the meat, and I spit out the bones. Unfortunately, there is always one that disguises itself so well within the meat that you don't realize it is a bone and you swallow it. The bone may get stuck there and you need something stronger to help get it down like water and a piece of bread. In this case for me, that bone went down smoothly, and I would never have known it was something that I should have gotten rid of. He stuck around disguised as something to keep instead.

There were many red flags, but the help I sought after was the blood of Jesus, the living water to help me cope through them. Besides, He is the one who sent him, this is just fear from my past, I should not make him pay for something he had not done, right?! He knew everything, there was no way he would hurt me. I found so many signs and reasons to walk away, but I could not. This was my angel, he has looked past all my flaws, why can't I look past his?

So, I did.

Once I questioned him about something that didn't sit right in my spirit, yet he gave me such an amazing response. I was like girl, don't you push him away. Friends would say the same. Everyone loved him who I introduced him to. They'd say, "It's you, not him." I would find myself not responding to what I saw were problems because everything was a problem for me. So, I had to humble myself and give him a little wiggle room. I needed to give him time to adjust to being in a relationship again.

I was a serial-situationshiper for the lack of a better word. He was not; he just worked at lot. He doesn't have small children, so there is no drama. I thought to myself

"Be patient with him because he has been patient with you." And I was. I talked to myself and prayed myself away from walking out of the door on multiple occasions.

"You have always been the one to leave, do something different if you want something different," is what I kept telling myself. I became less opinionated and less vocal and even more of a prayer warrior, not against him but *for* him. I mean a sanctified wife sanctifies an unsanctified husband, right? I wanted to be in practice now, something I had not learned to do previously. It was working.

He was quick to apologize; we didn't argue nor raise our voices at each other. He was always calm and would say "Baby, I love you, I won't hurt you."

He would take me shopping, send me cash, or ship me something: flowers, chocolates, or something for the kids, SOMETHING! This would melt my heart and he knew it. It became our thing, and I loved how he loved me. I again wanted for NOTHING, and he paid for EVERYTHING. My son became his son (again, my son's dad had passed). I could pay for nothing with him and if I did, he would reimburse me.

One time he even threatened to take me to court when I didn't want

to talk to him anymore as friends. He said, "You can stop talking to me, but don't take my son from me."

It was just amazing to have a man to fight for me as well as a child of mine that he had no pleasure in making. Even with all of that, something was not right in my spirit about him, I just could not figure it out. It was something familiar about him. What I know now is that I recognized the spirit in him.

We traveled together, he stayed over at my place and was always respectful. He was, in my Gena voice, "MY MANNN!!" (Gena from Martin).

He stayed consistent and it was three months of joy. A long-time friendship had turned into a lifetime love story. It was the happiest I had ever been. He catered to my every need: he cooked, cleaned, shopped, took our son off my hands, even after traveling on a long-distance job, working long hours. No literally!

We took a road trip for ten days, just he and I. Just the two of us had nothing to do but talk, eat and explore all the East and some of the

West Coast. It was one of the things on my bucket list. During these ten days it was a fairytale. He was so attentive, we prayed, did Bible study, and church service, the usual. We enjoyed dinner and wine, shopping and all the normal things we did. But his phone never rang. In previous conversations, I asked, where are your friends? He always had an amazing response because he was quick on his feet. "I have them, we just don't talk often."

"What about your family? I mean, no one calls you."

His response was, "Because now I am boring and into God, so I lost a lot of connections due to my changed lifestyle."

It was the same response all the time and each time I bought what he was selling. Until he was putting the TV together in the truck. I happened to look back and saw 'Jason Spencer' as his Wi-Fi. I saw that name before and asked, "Who is Jason Spencer?"

He responded, "Oh shoot, I selected the wrong one."

My eyebrows were raised.

I turned away to look at my phone as he searched for the "correct" Wi-Fi. The Holy Spirit said, "Look." Would you know 'Jason Spencer' happened to pop up gain. Well, you know my angel, always quick on his feet, gave some very sellable answers, only this time I wasn't buying. My angel was now shaking!

"Who is Jason Spencer?" What I was not yet aware of at the time is these were his same initials. But what I did pick up on is that he had emailed me years ago from a similar email address. While he was explaining it was yet again someone else's Wi-Fi and he just happened to keep selecting and putting in a password.

I was researching.

I went to my email and searched 'Jason Spencer.' Bingo! This 'Jason' had emailed me most recently in 2019 asking me had my son, 'our' son, arrived. I had not paid any attention to the 'Jason' thing, as 2019 was a horrific time for me. So many tests and trials came my way that I barely made it out as a sane individual, so an email address was the least of my concerns. But this email was now a huge concern in this season.

He fought me tooth and nail that he had never seen that Wi-Fi before. I asked him, as I am looking at this email on my phone, "Baby, I love you, please be honest." Again, he swore his innocence.

I became quiet, as I prayed. Because I felt the old me rising inside. We are in the middle of nowhere and this man is trying to convince me that it is the Wi-Fi for someone else. I began to think, well he did just get that phone as well as the TV, maybe it is connected.

"GIRL BYE!!" I snapped out of that, and I reminded him that he had emailed me from that type of name ten years ago. I also reminded him of what he told me, still not letting him know I was looking right at the emails. He parted his lips to look me straight in the eyes saying he never told me that he was signed into someone else's account by mistake at the fire department.

So convincingly, I almost second guessed what was staring me dead in my eyes on my screen. His voice would drop, his speech would slow, and his words became so soothing, telling me he never told me that. He tried to continue, even attempting to change the subject. Because like before, he was so good at doing so, it just had to work this time too. Even reminding me that we needed to go shopping for the things we missed on our many other trips to shop during that week.

I quickly interrupted, "Before you lie AGAIN, know I am looking right at the email. In your email, you CLEARLY stated that it was someone else's account, not once but twice. You used it by mistake; please think before you speak."

I'm still not looking at him, because I was going to SNAP if he lied again. This fool proceeded to tell me, "Okay, I lied."

I said, "No SUGAR," but I wanted to say the other "S" word. Instead, I let him speak. That now soothing voice just screams "BRACE YOURSELF, I'M ABOUT TO LIE" and that's exactly what he did. I looked at him crazy and asked, "Are you kidding me?" Is that the best you can come up with?"

He responded, "Well yes, because it is the truth. I'm sorry baby and I understand if you don't believe me because, I let a lie hurt us, but it is the truth." He continued, "That's why it's not good to lie because you must tell another to cover the first lie. But it was before us, and I should have been deleted it from my phone."

Prior to what seemed to be an amazing confession, I had also checked to see if that Wi-Fi would be available for my phone, you guessed it, it was there, clear and ready for a password. Now, part of his wonderful explanation, he never created the Wi-Fi, had never used it and just so happened to pop up with the phone. He was going to change the email address, so it won't pop up again. Whelp, while he was speaking, that Wi-Fi option was no longer an option for me.

I asked, "So you are going to delete the email so that Wi-Fi address won't show up again? Because you didn't create it, it was only attached to that email, right?"

He said, "Correct."

I told him that I don't believe him, but I would let it go. I did not want to make any more room for the enemy. Still thinking I can only see the Wi-Fi from the TV, he proceeded to delete the email. Can I tell you, later that night, 'Spencer Jason' jumped back up. I was disappointed, I knew he was still lying to me, and I told him. I pleaded with him during that now drawn-out vacation, to be honest with me. That I needed to be let in, he promised that it was nothing else and how terrible he felt for letting me down. Never again would he do so.

This still did not sit well with me. RED FLAGS were going up all over the place, and there were so many incidents that I had looked past because he was so convincing and would use God's name as collateral.

Sounded like a previous situation.

Unfortunately, I was ignorant, but God would not allow me to let this go. I continued asking about our future, and encouraging him more now than ever on the importance of letting me in. I expressed this to him previously during our cruise. While shopping for wedding rings, (that he initiated), only brought disappointment because his credit was not in place to make the purchase, but I understood. He preferred to do cash and promised we would be back for it. He planned for us to fly back for the ring from the US in the upcoming month. When that time came, well you know something came up.

What I know now is this was his deceptive way of giving himself more time to deceive me. But you know I dismissed it. Because I was not going to allow 'me' to talk myself out of this amazing man.

But back to this road trip which is actually three months since my birthday cruise. We had searched for ring after ring as he wanted me as his wife. However, he didn't want to get married if we didn't have the ring I wanted from the Bahamas. He stated that I deserved more. Plus, it was a beautiful ring so yes that worked before. I reminded him that this was not about a ring, it was about God. He agreed and said that he and God had been talking, and he already knew the next step.

"You do? So, God gave you a date?"

He said, "Yup, so I need you to let me, and God do what we do."

I smiled and said "OKAY!"

I mean, he *did* say God told him and all, so it must be true! Here I go again, the trick of the enemy specifically equipped for me *by* me.

I gave him the lead way. He knew I took the name of God seriously, and I thought others did as well.

The rest of that day we were on cloud nine. We were booed up, loved up and so excited about **US**. We went shopping, put some clothes on and went out on the town. He did it big that night as we do every time, he took me out. But this time, it was even better. He knew he was back in my good grace and wanted to celebrate the win.

The next morning, we were just a couple days before making it home from this 10-day road trip. We went to a nice breakfast and were ready for the day. However, I had a dream. God was trying to tell me something, I just didn't know what, so I shared it with him. In short, the dream consisted of us being in a car, I was the driver and he the passenger. Suddenly, a bike rider came and hit the car on the passenger side where he sat. I can recall in the dream noticing we were about to fly in the air. I grabbed the car with one hand to control it so the impact wouldn't be as dreadful, however it was. I had been thrown out of the car, was hurt pretty badly, and he was nowhere to be found.

I remember in the dream seeing my body on the ground. I was literally standing over my own body. My eyes were moving, and I could see I was breathing but clearly, I was unconscious. I recall the medic asking those around, "Has she ever been awake?" and I immediately, responded to the question about me, "YES," before waking from the dream.

He didn't know what to make out of it, so he dismissed it. But I was uneasy, and God was speaking. After prayer, I received my answer, and it was confirmed by a good sister in Christ. I was no longer awake, I was losing control of my inner voice, the Holy Spirit. I was so busy trying to 'save' us that I lost *me*. If I continued to deny the voice within (Holy Spirit) it would kill me because I was being disobedient.

Immediately, I repented, and I asked God for guidance about this. I pleaded for him to speak louder than ever before and that's what He did. It's what He had been doing, I simply needed to listen and shut out the other voices.

Later that week, I noticed a tatt that I had been seeing for years, but why was this so prevalent today? That night, I asked what his daughter's name was again. He confirmed what was on his arm. Immediately, I knew he was lying. It was the first time in ten years that I questioned it, but it was a vital piece of this puzzle.

The next morning, I went to him again, "Baby, I love you. You have loved me and my children, but you keep me at a distance from your world, why? "What are you hiding?"

Once again, he declared his innocence and said that he wants us to get married soon and next month we will go see his family. He insisted we go to one of my favorite breakfast spots, Iron Rooster, before that we went shopping for me and 'our' son. However, this was nice, but at this point, I'm uncomfortable. I was tired of being nice, it was time to be kind.

I couldn't confirm it, but my inner voice was not resting on this 'name' story. So, I began to follow the breadcrumbs. I told myself until this is settled, we are not going on another trip, and he was not welcome in my home again. I am UNCOMFORTABLE with all these years of friendship turned into LOVE.

What is going on?

The Holy Spirit spoke and continued speaking. I continued to listen as well as acted on what was being said instead of dismissing the clues. I now had concrete evidence, so I called him, and pleaded with him.

"Please, my love, let me in, I need you to be honest, we are all flawed

just be honest with me. Who is on the tattoo?"

He Immediately responded, "My daughter."

For a second, I began questioning these facts that I had. "Is he telling the truth?" But that inner voice stepped in, "BABY, PLEASE!!" I exclaimed. I simply wanted to hear the truth from him, although I already knew the answer. I felt like how God must feel with us, He simply want us to confess our sins, even though He knows them.

Yet, my love stuck to his story and asked, "Where is this coming from, Princess?"

Princess is a good friend of mine that too had some concerns about why he was taking so long to marry me and making an excuse about a ring. She had made her concerns to him, yet still he stuck to his guns. I am so glad he was over the phone not in my presence.

"Jane Jane, WHO IS SHE?"

He was quiet.

"She is your DAUGHTER, RIGHT?!?!"

He was still quiet.

I said "I know someone who knows your daughter. Her name is not

the name that is on the tattoo?"

He softly said "no!"

You have told me for years that it's your daughter, even showing me the tatt the other night, when that name is indeed your ex, RIGHT?" I asked, "WHY have you lied to me all these years," crying now, "I let you in, into my home, my heart, my family, why me?" Before he could answer, I firmly said, "And you're still married, RIGHT!?!"

He was caught, and because he didn't know the source or what I knew, he answered "umhmm!"

I screamed "WHYYYYYYYYYYY?? HOWWWWW could you do this to me, to us? I asked you OVER AND OVER, and you made me think I was crazy! You have been lying to me for YEARS, WHO ARE YOU!?!?"

He stated "Baby, let me explain!"

"EXPLAIN!?!?!? I have been BEGGING you to EXPLAIN for YEARS, now that you are caught, you want to EXPLAIN? You know what I have been through, you PROMISED to protect me, you said God sent you! YOU ARE EVIL, may God have mercy on you!"

I then hung up the phone. It was bittersweet because I had confirmed he was a calculated LIAR. He would do and say ANYTHING to protect his story, even if it meant hurting me, his LIE was protected!

I called my mom, "Mom, he is married, I knew something was not right."

"What are you going to do?" she asked.

I told her, "It's nothing I *can* do; I'm DONE, he has been deceiving me since we met years ago, I can't even be his friend now!"

The next day, I woke up with joy because again, I was *not* crazy at all. I was finally obedient to God and not this LIAR. Again, he simply wanted to explain how a small lie became a greater one and he should have been honest. I told him that he doesn't have an honest bone in his body and that he will suffer because he lost a GOOD thing. He begged for forgiveness, that is what he deserves, and it is the only way I will receive forgiveness. But forgiveness does not mean he has to be a part of my life.

I cried all day; I was in disbelief. We were planning to marry the next year, we were planning to move to Orlando, now everything changed because he LIED, constantly. I will heal quickly, but the hardest part of it all is my son, who had already lost his deceitful father while in my womb. This man knew this and helped me sort through it only to do the same thing. He lost not just one dad, but two. This could have all been avoided, had my angel not been a devil in disguise.

I know now to always trust my gut. And to try the spirit by the spirit. This was the same test I had failed a few years back, thankfully no one had to physically die in the process because now, I listened. Better later than never. Nevertheless, I was once again disobedient and there are consequences for disobedience. Though I pray to eventually get back up on that bike, I will be more selective of the path I take to get to it. I will also be more mindful of the meat I consume because again, the bones that should have been spit out, may pass as meat, and just might eventually choke the life out of me, if not careful.

There is nothing like disappointing God by falling into the same tricks of the enemy. Thankfully, we are in Christ Jesus and in Him there is no condemnation when we seek to please the spirit instead of the flesh. The word says God's grace is sufficient so don't beat yourself up. Just take this time to write those experiences down, knowing eventually it all will work for your good.

Chapter 17

DEAR FUTURE HUSBAND, "DON'T COME TO ME TALKING ABOUT GOD."

I am angry, mad, and bitter. The next man who comes to me talking about God, will probably get punched in his face. Not literally as I'm not a violent person, I am a woman of God. I'm just so sick of this. Why do men use the name of God to get what they want?

I never knew breaking up could feel like this. This hit differently. The first thing I did was feel the relief that my intuitions were right. The second thing was get my nails done.

It's what he would do when I was sad, pamper me. The third thing I did was cry because I didn't just lose my man, I lost my friend too. The fourth thing I did was became ANGRY because I'm used to controlling when I leave someone, in this case, I was forced because he was not honest. The fifth thing I did was experience regret. "How could you have been so STUPID? You ignored the red flags." The sixth thing I did was CRIED, a lot!

The seventh thing I felt was EMBARRASSMENT, eighth thing I felt was JOY that I had the strength to walk away even though I would lose so much, physically, emotionally and financially. Ninth thing was loneliness, "Did I overreact? Should I give him another chance? Who will I vacation with now? Who will I talk to all day and all night? Who will I laugh with?"

The tenth thing I did was I reminded myself of how great I am. I began to recall that all we did together, I did before him and will continue to do now that his lies forced me to walk away! Here I go again, I did not trust the voice of God I had come to know as once again, I wanted to believe so much that this man was honest, believing his word over God's word. God was not pleased; I am once again dealing with the spirit of deception. This is due to the lack of having on the full armor of God, I gave the enemy a footing and once again, he ran with it. Lord help me!

***

I went to bed extremely heavy. I just could not process all that happened in the past three days. This must be a nightmare; not again. Another man of God has come in and stolen my joy, he has taken my peace and grabbed a hold of my heart so tight and won't let go. His lies have me questioning my yesterday, shattered my today and destroyed my tomorrow.

We had so many plans. We were doing everything according to the plans of God; I insisted, and he obliged. What happened to us? I just did not understand. Where did I go wrong? The house was quiet, the questions and doubts in myself screamed louder and louder.

Tonight, is the hardest of the 'How do we go from this to that?!?!?' I have not been able to stop crying. What do I do with all the pictures, videos and gifts? Everything reminds me of him. My son keeps asking for him. My heart keeps yearning for him. The trash in the house is waiting for him to take it out. My gas tank is waiting for him to fill it up.

My hand is missing his tap when I even reach to pay, carry anything, or attempt to open a door. I didn't eat dinner because I am so used to him taking care of it. He took care of everything! Why couldn't he have taken better care of my heart, which is most important?

My iPad broke while we were on the road earlier in the month. I told him not to buy me another, but he did. Yet another reminder of him. I want to hate, but I can't. I will not open myself back up to him. I didn't and don't deserve his poor choices in deception. He confesses his faults and asks for forgiveness, it's granted because I want God to forgive me.

I went into prayer for forgiveness myself, simply for not adhering to the voice of God. Like him, I got caught up in what he was *saying* was God instead of tapping into the inner voice inside of me which is the Holy Spirit. I just wanted to believe he was hearing from God, but the Bible says not to put your trust in man, yet that's exactly what I did. So, we both were disobedient, and disobedience is sin. Once I grasped that concept, my heart felt lighter. Jesus forgave me, I forgave this man, and the burden was gone.

I slept well.

I woke up to **Hebrew 5:7**, it spoke on the High Priest (Christ) was offered as a great sacrifice for our sins and if we simply cry out with a strong cry, prayer and supplications that we are saved from death. I stood in my kitchen and as I played gospel, each song that came on was a follow-up to what God was speaking. Song by song, my father was speaking to me, and I felt such joy in my heart. No longer did the enemy have me in a place of anger, bitterness or sorrow. I was made free in Christ Jesus.

Then I received an extremely long text from my 'supposed' to be future husband. Though he had apologized before, I believe he had truly been convicted. He pleaded to God and revealed all his deception that kept him in bondage. I thought it would make me angrier with him. Instead, my heart softened for him. I knew he was also a victim of that sneaky devil and like me, he needed grace. He needed to know that the same savior that died for me, died for Him as well.

I was able to comfort him in his now discomfort caused by his own actions. He celebrated the God in me once again. He reminded me about how I am truly one of God's anointed ones and how deeply grateful he is to have known me. He knew we would not be together again, but he was comforted in seeing the God in me allow him to give his friend back.

God has gotten the glory; the kingdom has won back a precious gem and gained another. We as followers of Christ must represent Him properly, being the salt of the earth, bringing life to every dead situation in our lives. Showing others that there is nothing that God won't FORGIVE us for if only we seek it. Just as we are to give forgiveness to others, even if we don't think they deserve it. That's practicing **Ephesians 4:32**.

What I learned from this experience is what most of us as Christ followers don't understand. I was so busy looking at the wrong he did to me that I could not see the wrong I was doing to **God**. We are often so focused on the pain someone has caused us that we don't see how we made room for the enemy. I will speak more on this in an upcoming volume which I learned just a few weeks ago. What I just learned is that it applies here. It was that which was in me (inner me) that activated the enemy.

"I'm hurt. How could they do that to me?"

We become victims of what we created. In this case, if I had been more trusting in my relationship with Christ, I would not have been so distracted by the religion in him. Boy that hit hard. But it's part of this process of growing up in Christ.

Can you relate to this experience you just read? Take a moment and pause, reflect and write it out.

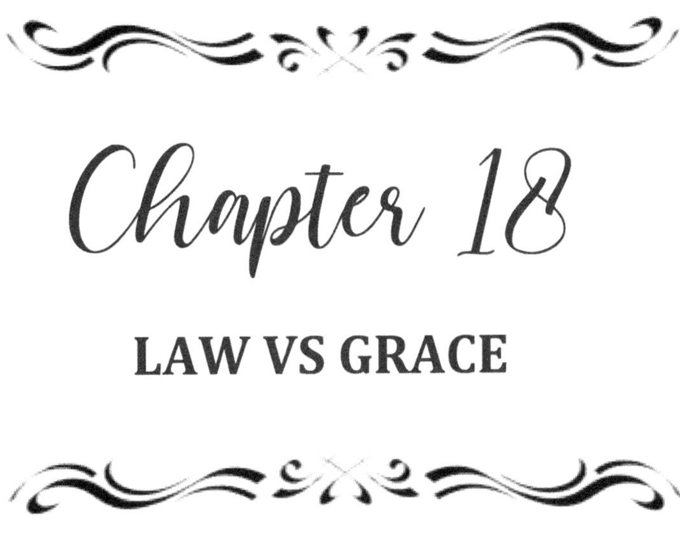

Chapter 18

LAW VS GRACE

Understanding the Sabbath had been pressing in my spirit for a few months. This occurred after over a year of becoming stuck so to speak with an assignment for "The Spiritual Night Cap." This was a segment I was moved to begin to minister to the people. The foundation had been built and established on **Isaiah 61**, being called to preach the 'Good News of Salvation.' I was in no way equipped to do so, but I was reminded that God does not call the equipped, but instead He equips the 'called.'

I went forward with pure obedience. I would move according to what the Holy Spirit moved me to speak on each evening. Things were going well until I reached the 10 commandments in Exodus.

Each night I was breaking down ever so gently a very simple understanding of each command, 'Thy Shall Not...'

I was in a great groove with the assistance of the Holy Spirit. That is until I reached the 4th commandment: "Remember the Sabbath and Keep it Holy."

This seemed simple enough. Like previous nights, the Holy Spirit would guide me right through. Only on this night, I could not proceed with my teachings. Well, I could have, however, I was not clear on what I understood about 'Keeping the Sabbath holy' nor the origin of it.

As the week went on, I wanted to KNOW! I was baffled, yet I proceeded to at least try to honor it, I mean it as simple as not doing any work right?

WRONG!

At that time, all I wanted to do is show my love for God. In the book of John it states, "If you love me, keep my commandments."

I wanted to obey.

I told everyone I am honoring the Sabbath. Anytime they wanted me to do things I may have done previously during Sabbath, no matter who it was, I would not participate. Some stated that the Sabbath was Sunday and some Saturday. I was confused, but I decided to trust what I understood, and that the Sabbath was Saturday.

It was going great, Friday sunset to Saturday sunset. I got the kids involved as the scripture stated no one works right? Even when Jesus went to heal someone, He was challenged by the Pharisees that no work was to be done on the Sabbath day. But Jesus so ever gently explained His way was the exception to the rule.

Of course, understanding isn't truly what they were after, instead they were more interested in tripping Jesus up, a challenge if you will. It reminds me of the movement of Satan in the garden of Eden when he told Eve, in so many words she would not surely die. Instead, according to this snake, God did not want her seeing things as He saw it. But Eve fell for the tricks of the enemy.

Unlike Eve, Jesus who is the word, knew and saw the deception a mile away and was ready. Sort of where I found myself, trying to differentiate between what the Word (Jesus) said and that the world was saying, only I truly wanted understanding. I asked people of God, and I personally went to God myself. I still had no clear understanding on how to truly honor the Sabbath. I did my best and opened myself for God to do the rest.

Months later, I had Pastors tell me that Jesus is the Sabbath, so we don't need to rest as He is our rest. Though there is validity in that statement that can be referenced in various places in the Bible. One of my favorites is **Matthew 11:28-29**, however that did not sum up the Sabbath for me and keeping it Holy.

I had more questions like, "Why would it be a day referenced in the Bible for rest, and why would it say no work?"

I then became familiar with 'grace vs law,' and that you cannot be under both. Jesus came to fulfill the law because apparently, we as fleshly beings could not. If we are in Christ Jesus, we are under grace, no longer the law, true. Still, there were some unanswered questions for me.

"Lord," I would ask, "Please help me understand."

Months went by and still no clarity, so I continued honoring the Sabbath as I was. God had not spoken differently to me, so I will stay the course until He does.

One evening in Bible study, the 10 commandments were addressed, and it was said that by honoring the two, like Jesus stated, we are honoring them all. I am really confused now. Why would all these commandments be written, only for us to follow two?

Love your God with all your heart and all your soul as well as love your neighbors. If that is all we have to worry about? As when you honor those two commandments, you have honored them all.

As I was driving in my car one evening and months later. I was still in search of the truth. "God where are you in this, help me," I thought to myself. In that moment, it was relayed to me to really break down what these scriptures meant. I made several calls to people I trusted in the word so we could dissect these scriptures together. Besides, the word says when two or more are gather in Jesus that He is in the midst. I needed Jesus. Only they too agreed that rest is in Christ. There was no dispute there for me, I wanted to know and understand how that related to the Sabbath.

I began speaking as it was being downloaded to me by the Holy Spirit. There was a question posed. Do the scriptures state that just because we are no longer under the law and under grace that we are excused to continue to sin? The answer was and is **NO** for me. Paul puts it this way in scripture **Romans 6:1–2** "What shall we say then? Shall we continue in sin, that grace may abound? God forbid. How shall we, that are dead to sin, live any longer therein?" He was teaching that God's grace is not permission to continue living in sin. Grace saves us, transforms us, and calls us higher. Here is another **Titus 2:11–12** "For the grace of God that bringeth salvation hath appeared to all men, teaching us that, denying ungodliness and worldly lusts, we should live soberly, righteously, and godly, in this present world." **So,** Grace is not just forgiveness, it is also instruction and transformation.

I began to explain what the Holy Spirit was breaking down to me. Those two commandments, though I now understood why they cover all the scriptures, I wanted to verbalize it. The only way ALL the commandments would be covered by these two is if we practiced fully what is being asked of us. If we truly love God with ALL our heart and all our soul, we would already be following the 10 commandments. We would not put no other God before the one true God. We wouldn't make any graven images of Him; how could we, we never seen him, so that would be other Gods we are creating? Our love for God just would not move us to want to steal, kill, lie, etc. And if we are truly loving our neighbors, we wouldn't want to cause them any harm out of fear and the love of both them and God. We would not bear false witness, we would not commit adultery, nor would we want something someone else had. Instead, celebrate what they had.

Sabbath falls right under these two as well. Yes, we hand over anything that causes us stress to Christ in exchange for a lighter burden in our spirit in trying to do it ourselves. However, there is a physical rest, that's the no work portion of this, we are to set aside a day in honor of our salvation to fully focus on righteousness, not work or deeds but replenishment. I later came to realize and better explain to others that Christ coming does not mean we no longer honor the commandments. Instead, Christ came that we would not seek salvation through the law Now we have been given grace and by grace, we receive righteousness. Now I have a better understanding of Christ needing to die on the cross, we simply cannot do it in our own strength.

I recall having COVID, and because I was so used to doing, I simply felt like I had to keep doing. If you have ever had COVID, you may have experienced similar symptoms no appetite, no taste, no strength, just complete weakness and exhaustion. Yet even in that condition, I kept pushing myself. I remember practically crawling down the stairs just to tend to the children and make sure they had eaten. What I did not know was that a neighbor had already brought food, so they were fine. My spiritual parents had also dropped off supplies, so everything was already taken care of.

Instead of allowing myself to go back upstairs and rest, I continued trying to clean. I heard the Holy Spirit telling me to get in bed, but how could I? In my mind, I had too much to do. Still wanting to be obedient, I slowly dragged myself back upstairs. That is when I was told the bathtub was clogged; not the toilet, but the tub. I grabbed the plunger and began trying to fix it. There was dark, black sewage-looking water sitting in the tub from only God knows where. This had never happened before, but there I was.

The more I plunged, the harder I worked, and the weaker I became. I was trying to balance myself just to gain enough strength to continue, but nothing was changing except the tears running down my face. Finally, from complete exhaustion, I collapsed onto the floor. In pain, I cried out to the Lord, and immediately, the dark water suddenly became clear and drained from the tub on its own. And so did my understanding. In that moment, I was reminded that apart from God, we can do nothing. This would have been the perfect time for me to cast all my cares upon Him, but instead I tried to carry everything in my own strength until I was finally forced to seek Him completely.

Understand that there is a difference between physical rest required for Sabbath and spiritual rest required for the soul. Physical rest is when your body recovers from work, stress, or exhaustion through sleep, relaxation, eating properly, or simply slowing down. Spiritual rest, however, is deeper. It is the peace that comes from trusting God, surrendering burdens to Him, and no longer striving in your own strength. Physical rest restores the body, but spiritual rest restores the soul.

From a biblical perspective, my experience with COVID connected deeply to the principle of Sabbath. I was physically weak, exhausted, and clearly in need of rest, yet because I was so used to doing and carrying responsibility, I felt like I still had to keep going. Even when the Holy Spirit instructed me to get in bed, there was something in me that struggled to stop because I believed there was still too much to do.

But what I did not realize was that God had already made provision. The children had food. Supplies had already been dropped off. What I was trying to carry in my own strength had already been covered by God through the help of others. Instead of allowing myself to rest, I kept doing.

That is what Sabbath teaches us. Sabbath is not just about stopping work; it is about trusting God enough to stop striving. It is the spiritual discipline of remembering that we are not the source, God is. When we refuse to rest, we can sometimes reveal the hidden belief that everything depends on us. But Sabbath reminds us that God is still working, providing, and sustaining even when we are still.

The clogged tub and dark water became a picture of what happens when we keep pushing beyond our strength while ignoring God's instruction. Sabbath is not laziness. Sabbath is obedience. It is faith in action. It is saying, "Lord, I trust You enough to rest." Sometimes the most spiritual thing we can do is stop, be still, and let God be God.

Unlike in the Old Testament days, there was no grace, only condemnation. However, in the New Testament, there is no condemnation in us who seek after the Spirit and not after the flesh. This means, the more we seek after the guidance from the Holy Spirit, even if we fall short of the mark while pushing forward, we have grace to carry us through. That brings us to **Matthew 6:33** *"But seek ye first the kingdom of God, and his righteousness; and all these things shall be added unto you."*

This scripture is a reminder from Jesus Christ to place God first above worry, possessions, status, and earthly concerns. When we prioritize God's will, His righteousness, and His way of living, He promises to provide what we truly need on this journey of growing up in Christ.

Can you imagine having to follow all those commandments to the letter to receive righteousness? It was impossible! Glory be to God for the sacrifice in Christ. Had it not been for Christ, we would not have the grace to cover us for our sins to help us in the times we may fall short in our salvation.

This gives me joy to know that my past, current and future sins have already been forgiven. Because of this gift, I do not have strive to live sinless, as I seek after a true Relationship with Christ, God will do it for me as I surrender my will for His to be done.

Self-Reflection

Time to pause. What are your thoughts after reading this chapter? What is your understanding of grace vs law? Please take a moment to reflect on those times and use space below to share your own experience.

____

____

____

____

____

____

____

____

____

____

____

____

Chapter 19

A TIME FOR ORDER

As soon as I grasped the understanding of the law and grace, another need for understanding was under way. They say once you pass one test, another comes. I guess this is what the scripture means concerning enduring to the end as there are experiences to build or strengthen our faith. But my God, I just needed a moment; may I please come up for air for a little bit?

Not at all.

This thing continued to press on my spirit and would not let me go.

That same night, I was asked to help with a church service; immediately I said yes. I figured I may be needed to help with the music or something behind the scenes, not the case. I was asked to give a message in the Pastor's absence. Excited, I said yes. Well, I just received the breakdown of rest and Sabbath, maybe this is what Holy Spirit will have me speak about.

Days went by and I still had not been clear. Yet I kept seeing **1 Corinthians 14**. I was still not quite clear about it as a good friend had mentioned it to me earlier that week in need of clarification. I went in a bit baffled on why this person could not see this scripture so clearly. When I read it, it was immediately clear to me.

I began to explain it and then I stumbled upon vs 34, "A woman is to be silent in the church," in so many words. I had seen this scripture before but this night, I could not rest immediately. I heard the Holy Spirt say, "You are not to give this message." At this point, it was in a few hours.

I was perplexed as I had already committed, besides what is the harm? I had given a message many times previously, so I pleaded, "Lord speak to me so I may understand your word better."

Besides the word does say, "In all things, get an understanding." Don't get me wrong, I would not move forward regardless.

However, I needed clarity on why I could not go forward with a message for the people in the church.

The Holy Spirit was silent; I had no response other than NO! That was enough for me but if I may be honest, I did not like the silent treatment nor the lack of understanding. Nevertheless, I obeyed.

As I settled in the Holy Spirit's full statement in "NO," and having to now tell the pastor, I was quite uneasy. This took me back to my childhood. You may be able to relate to being told "no" as a child. If you were like me, you'd ask "why not?" If the adults around you were like those around me, you'd either get the silent treatment or a sharp answer of "Because I said so."

"How unfair," I'd think to myself. But that was my sign to leave it alone.

The day went on, and I began to get a clearer revelation on why I could not give the message. Paul spoke in Corinthians that a woman is not allowed to speak in church. I reasoned with myself that this could not be true as the scripture says, "There is no Jew nor Greek, bound nor free, male nor female, we are one in Christ," **Galatians 3:28**. This verse was explained to me and others that this opened the rule Paul stated in **1 Corinthians**.

"So how could this be so," I thought to myself.

I read over **1 Corinthians** several times then back to **Galatians** as well as other cross-referenced scriptures, asking the Holy Spirit to give me a revelation. And just like that, as I continued to study, a light went off. The book of Galatians is not spoken from a physical perspective, instead the spirit, our souls. Once in Christ Jesus, gender, origin, status etc. does not matter. Jesus is only concerned about the soul when it comes to salvation.

No matter who we are, as **John 3:16** so wonderfully exclaims, 'whomsoever' believes, shall not parish, but have everlasting life. That took me back to 1 Corinthians, "What are you saying here, Lord?"

He was speaking about the order in the Kingdom. It is the rule that women should be quiet in the church not teaching and not heading men. Not because we weren't able due to lack of skills or quality, but instead order. I was then taken over to chapter 11 where I was clearly given the exception to *when* a woman can speak in church.

This blew my mind, it broke down the order: God over Jesus, Jesus over the husband, the husband over the wife. Only then if there is the proper order being displayed, then a woman may use her gifts in the church. Still not being head over the man, instead the man over the woman. Not in a manner of control or disrespect as the scripture tells the man, to LOVE your wife as Christ loves the church. Like Christ being obedient and only teaching and leading us according to the word of God, so shall the husband lead and teach the wife. She is the help mate, she can be in support of the husband and a strong voice in her home, but under the husband.

I said, "Well I am not married." But I was reminded that I am, in the spirit, I am the Bride of Christ, and I missed the order. I said yes to the Pastor *before* clearing and being approved by my spiritual husband. I didn't understand, why did I have to go through all of this to understand a 'NO?' Why didn't God simply state that to me.

Well, authority and order in the home is something I have been struggling with for as long as I can remember. The word says that we will be given the desires of our heart. My desire is to be married, no truly in the word. I had been married in the world but never understood the covenant of marriage as I was not in relationship with Christ.

My goal is not to make the same mistakes I have made previously; God knows that. Therefore, I am being taught through relationship with Christ how to be a submissive wife to my husband. Many would say, "We aren't living in caveman times anymore." My response to that is that there has been such a disorder that even the most devoted believers are out of sorts and not following the order of the kingdom. This is why there is such a high rate of divorce in the church. As well as conflict between man and woman in the workplace, the home and in the church. We must build a stronger relationship with Christ so like me, someone who once in such disobedience to order, now marvel at the idea to practice it, perfect it and display in the marriage God has for me.

Self-Reflection

We have come to the end of another chapter. What does Kingdom order look like to you? Tell me about a time you have struggled with the order of God, or maybe you are still struggling and trying to understand, or just maybe you have it figured out. Reference the word of God and share it right here in the space provided.

MEL SPEARS

Chapter 20

THE ROOTS OF THE MATTER

After multiple weeks of seeing my son struggle to breathe due to a head cold, it eventually went away but I was wondering, "Why is this back?"

My son's breathing during those weeks had become increasingly worst. I just didn't understand. My son was having a difficult time breathing, which is necessary for any of us to live. As I sadly and helplessly watched my son struggle for breath daily, I was slowly losing hope.

The first night went by and although there were no symptoms of cold, he struggled to breathe all night. He could not sleep, nor could I. I was hurting seeing my son in such a struggle.

A week prior I was mad at God, I could not pray any more, I didn't want to read the word, but however, I could worship. So, worship is what I did. I sang and cried in thanks and the songs were very encouraging. One of my go to songs is by Maverick City: God Will Work It Out. It always gets me through. And though it helped make me feel better at that moment, the same struggle presented itself that night.

After a sleepless night and feeling I was being ignored by God and even being tested yet again with the same test, I was mad. I have asked for what I need to learn during this season yet again, I thought we made it past this. I had given testimony of You healing Jeremiah, how is it I tell people now, that that was a lie because we are going through the same challenges. How are these tests back?

I began to ask myself, "Were the doctors, right?" "Will Jeremiah need surgery after all?" Lord don't make me out to be a liar in your name. So, I was confused. As I got up my worship became my focus, I could no longer look at my child struggling to breathe. During my worship, though I could not pray nor read the word that morning, God was getting the glory. The Holy Spirit spoke, and I was reminded as I stated in the 'My Son Suffered' chapter, that this is Gods son, not mine. He was only on loan to me, and I was chosen to be his mom. He still belongs to God and what belongs to God, He will not forsake.

I cried in thanksgiving as well as in forgiveness for second guessing God. No, my testimony wasn't in that moment of healing my child, but He is a child of God and He takes care of His. I was moved and at peace.

Up until today, earlier this morning as I watered and nurtured my severely dying plants, I kept hearing the Holy Spirit say, 'The roots.'

When the roots are good, the plants can always be revived. I thought nothing more of this and figured it was as simple as that and just a continuation of "the potting" chapter. It wasn't until the evening that I was writing this when it became very clear.

Last night was another sleepless night. It was another early morning in prayer trusting and believing God but feeling I could not trace Him. I prayed; Jeremiah woke fine in the AM, so the day went as normal. Again, here in the evening, Jeremiah is asleep, and the struggle is even greater to the point of bringing me to tears. I kept saying I didn't understand. God I just pleaded with you this morning. I reminded Him of His word in tears, "Lord you said

"Speak to that mountain and it shall be moved." You also said *"Ask and it shall be given, seek and it shall be found knock and it shall be opened."*

Huge tears fell from my eyes, "I have spoken and believed in You for everything I had prayed and asked You for, because it is Your word. But where are You God? Did I do something? Why are you not answering?"

I went as far as believing I had been turned over to a reprobate mind (turned over to my sin). In agony, I asked the Lord, "Is that why you don't hear me?"

I thought about King Saul after being disobedient to God and God no longer heard him, "Is this where I am God?"

I cried even harder.

"This was not where I want to be. Lord, I have been asking you, I have pleaded for peace as your word says despite not understanding, why have you turned from me? Why do I not have peace."

I searched for myself and cried. I got up to start moving and I cried out to my love at the time. It's Sabbath and He said, "Rest."

"How can I rest seeing my son like this?" I told him, as I cried, "This is why non-believers are not convinced and doubt there is a God or that He is for them. How do I get around this?"

I believed God but it made me mad that He wasn't hearing me, and I didn't even know why. I want to tell you the good news of the Lord, but this is not good news. I'm tired.

I cried and got busy in the kitchen. So, I walked into the kitchen, and I got busy in there just to keep myself from focusing on my son's struggle. Still crying from heart break and mere disappointment in God, I just began watering my plants. They too are my babies, but I have not tended to them lately. I thought I'd take time to give them some TLC.

In the process of watering them as I walked over to the island just fumbling around, I opened the drawer. I truly have no idea what made me open it. I was watering plants, nothing in the drawer would help me with that task. Once the drawer was opened, I noticed there was a huge meat cleaver. Where it was positioned in the drawer startled me. I immediately thought, "What if Jeremiah opened this drawer? The knife is so sharp that even the slightest wrong touch would severely cut his hand."

Out of concern, I turned the cleaver over and pushed it to the furthest part of the drawer from the opening. I did not want it to cut any of the children's hands. Once I moved the sharp object, I noticed something I had been frantically looking for since I returned home from vacation. I looked through everything in that drawer as well as the others because I knew it was there. I had even looked earlier that day. But it was nowhere to be found. Once I stopped stressing over the tool that morning, I knew was there, and moved what was sharp that could have caused harm , what I was looking for was right there. I just needed to take my mind off my pain from what I *could* see and focus on other areas that needed care.

Isn't that like God?

The more we stress, the less likely He is to respond. Not because He is ignoring us, but to strengthen us to believe that no matter what it looks like, he is always there. Continuing to cry or losing faith does not help, we simply need to redirect the focus on what we *can* do, instead of what He is *not* doing.

In the mist of that, this beautiful revelation came to me. I smiled and went on to water my plants. As I picked up the water bottle, I was drawn over to this one plant. The first one that I saw looked so beautiful. After all this time, it still had life, the leaves were very full and a beautiful green color. It just looked like there was so much life there. Yet the very twin, instead, was just the opposite. It looked like it had taken on so much. So much had to be cut as well as cleaned from the plant. It was clearly suffering. The plant had water tubes, and the water was gone. So, it gave me hope that as dead as it looks, there is clearly life because its healthy twin had no watering glass tubes.

How is it the one that is not thirsty, does not need water, yet seems to have so much life? But the one that has water fed into it looks like it is dead. The one with water has no visual signs of life but is fully functioning where the eyes cannot see because it's drinking. This is due to its foundation, the 'root' of the plant.

The Holy Spirit reminded me that though it *looks* dead, it is instead full of life and being revived from the bottom up. This answered my question concerning Jeremiah. To the eyes he is suffering but to the spiritual eye God is still working in him. He may not look like it but there is still lots of life in him.

I smiled and said, "Thank you Jesus."

Since I have had these plants, God's been using them to minister to me. I have four plants as of now. I originally had five, but I wasn't as plant friendly as I am now. What I have now are two Peace Lilly's, a Cat Palm tree and one other large plant. The cat palm is the one when I purchased the plants, it was unknowingly in horrible condition. Like it had no life left, just like my Peace Lily at this time. After a while, what I learned is that it was pot bound. The pot was too small for the roots to continue to grow properly. It outgrew its environment causing the roots to wrap around the inside of the pot and sort of being in its own prison.

Had I known what the name of the plant was before purchasing, it would have never made it home with me. Cats of any sort just aren't something I enjoy. But despite its name, this plant would be the one to challenge me for the better, like Jeremiah, it requires a lot of TLC and I am the one to do so.

When I walked back into the room where Jeremiah had been sleeping, I realized I was no longer crying over him. God was very strategic again with redirecting my focus. The very thing I had to do with this Cat Palm, the very plant that I would not have chosen, chose me. I needed to continue to do that with Jeremiah.

My son sat up on the sofa, with the biggest smile on his face and I knew right then, it is well. Nothing changed in his breathing while sleeping at night, nevertheless, yet he woke up with joy. That's the evidence of God, when we get to the root of the matter. No matter how grim it looks, as long as our roots are grounded in Him, there is always life.

Share your experience where you have witnessed the hand of God move by the activation of your faith. Use the space below as well as the empty page provided if needed, to elaborate on that experience

Chapter 21

ONLY FEW ARE CHOSEN...

I went to the theatre to see the 'Back to Black' movie about the late Amy Winehouse who passed away some years back at the very young age of 27. I didn't finish the movie, but as I sat waiting for my meal, I wanted to know what the technical cause of death was. According to Amy's dad's interview with People Magazine, the medical term for her death was declared as alcohol poisoning. My personal term based off what I heard in her music and witnessed from the story line, young Amy died of heartbreak.

Amy wanted to be chosen by someone, but her toxic lifestyle prevented her from having good relationships. This caused her life to spiral out of control due to her outlook on people and their impact on her life.

In that moment, I began to reflect on my own life. What self-sabotaging activities have I succumbed to daily? If I were to die today, what will be the medical term for my death and what will be the thoughts of my Heavenly Father?

Like most of us, the blueprint of Amy's family life had been what seemed to be a cycle of trauma, chaos, and lots of pain in the form of disappointments. She had no ability to choose herself and those who were around could not guide her to a better sense of purpose. Amy in my opinion, viewing from of my relationship with Christ, chose death for a lack of better words.

Carrying the weight of her mother and her father, Amy turned to sex, alcohol drugs, self-pleasures and superficial ways to block pain that really had nothing to do with her. She indulged in pleasures instead of healing her pain, which only deepened it. That deep hurt and self-hate craved for a harder drug. She went from a drink or two, to marijuana, to bottles of drinks at a time, to crack cocaine and God only knows what else. She placed what she had left over for a heart into a man who was in a sense as broken as she was because he had his own addictions and demons to fight.

This man was the one who she gave her heart and soul to. He was familiar, and he was just like her. He was the one she chased after, fought for and ultimately died for. Due to her lack of acceptance from people, she chose a different type of drug, a man instead of THE MAN. One who was merely flesh just as she was. One who bled and was flawed just as she was. Yet she trusted her all in him.

There was a line in the movie when she stated (he) Blake was trying to walk away from Amy's toxic behavior. She said that he was her heart, and her soul. Can you imagine how Christ felt? Not just with Amy but with **any** of us who chose those things that He has not chosen for us.

Isn't this how we move through life?

We put so much hope into man and things only to be let down as we are allowing ourselves to live out the blueprint of lives that often predated us based on the world and not the **word**. A life that began to torment us even before leaving and possibly entering our mother's womb.

I recall, according to the movie, Amy's only goal was to have a family. She wanted a baby, a family. Based off what? The need to feel loved?

Her life was out of control; she had not yet dealt with the generational curses that were haunting her daily. She didn't have the strength to break them in her life, so she was destined to pass the same torch she picked up on to her children. Her lack of ability to reproduce amongst other things in her life and relationship constantly turned to fleshly pleasures instead of seeking spiritual healing. A temporary fix instead of a lifestyle change.

Her delusions stemmed from such a broken background, a background that she chose to pick up the torch and carry out. She thought like many of us, bringing a child or even another person into these already daunting situations would somehow fix or heal her deep pain. She wanted to be loved by someone or something when deep down she could not love herself, yet she was seeking to give to others what she had not learned or been disciplined to give to herself.

Can you imagine if she simply believed, she could have, as the word says, cast her cares upon the Lord. Her outcome could have been a little different. God could have used all of what the enemy used for bad and made for good. Amy would have known she was already loved by love itself, a love greater than one she could ever imagine or ever be able to replace. Had she only believed she was loved by loved, she simply needed to decide to allow it.

As I rested that evening and reflected on my life, I thought about how in many ways I have been Amy. Unlike Amy, I believed and had cast some, but not ***all*** my cares upon the Lord. In that very moment, I had come to realize I too had been self-sabotaging. Not in the same instances as Amy, however the impact was the same. No, I hardly drank, no drugs ever and never been one to sleep around. However, due to the blueprint of my past and some of my own choices, I had deep unhealed pain. I lacked discipline and too had a record of choosing what had not been chosen for me. Like Amy I wanted a family and did what I thought I could to keep my family together. The one I had been given and the one I had chosen. Like Amy, my pain chose a path for me and for far too long I went along with that path, continuing the cycles of a past that had nothing to do with me instead of what was chosen for me, so I thought.

The book of Matthew says many are called but only few are chosen (**Matthew 22:14**). This plays out so vividly in my life, in Amy's life and in the lives of many of you. We are 'called' by so many people, having tons of followers, multiple friends, relationships and even family members. We have all kinds of worldly things that call us and we often choose. Out of ignorance or possibly rebellion, we put our all into them. We put our heart and soul into things and people who aren't even equipped to choose us, yet we choose them.

We are led to a path of destruction in many ways instead of following the one who chose us. Like many of you, I have been chosen. There has been a plan, the true blueprint that has been so carefully orchestrated for my life. Not the plans of my earthly father or mother and not based on the sins nor the generational curses that haunted my every waking moment. But a plan that my Heavenly Father so wonderfully crafted for my life. A plan specifically designed despite the sins of my ancestors, my parents or my own sins.

This plan is so eloquently described to us in the book of Jeremiah. **Jeremiah 29:11** lets us know that these plans are to prosper us, not to harm us, a plan for a brighter future. So, if there is something in our lives that contradicts that, we are going against God and His plans. We, like Amy, are walking into what could be a self-inflicted death as we are believing more of what the enemy says instead of what God said about us.

This is insanity.

Why wouldn't we make the decision to truly live out that plan, the plan God has for us? No, we are not God, we cannot see into the future or predict how it will play out. We serve a sovereign God, one who knows the past, present and future. He is the one who is the same God yesterday, today and forever more. Why would we not adhere to THE plan, play by play? There is no other reason outside of lack of belief.

The God we serve, He can help us with all our struggles. We simply need a mustard seed of faith according to the word, and He will do the rest. Who would not serve a God like that?

I wonder if Amy knew she had access to Him. Do you? *I do.*

Because of the access I have been granted, no longer will I give into the things of this world or the flesh which has and will continue to lead to self-sabotage. Unlike Amy, I still have a chance to officially break the chains of the world's blueprint on my life and follow the blueprint of God.

The good news is, so do you.

We have a choice. No matter how long we have been on a destructive path, we have choice. What do *you* choose? Will you continue a path of self-destruction, grieving the Holy Spirit? Or will you choose the path of everlasting life? I choose the one who chooses me. I choose life not death. I choose to live in the light no longer allowing the darkness to consume me. I choose to be free not in bondage of my sins. I choose Heaven over hell.

Because I cherish the choice to live, I will redirect my energy to *His* way, no longer my way. For instance, the same energy and effort I put into pleasing people or even myself, I will now put into my Savior. He is the only one who has sacrificed His life so I could live. He gave us the option to live and have eternal life; it's His only begotten son's blood that was shed on Calvary.

I choose to live and not die.

Self-Reflection

Here is your opportunity to reflect on this chapter and everything we discussed in this book. Do not take your journaling and reflections for granted, as this moment in time will pass you by, but can be revisited later.

Reflect, relate and release!

____

____

____

____

____

____

____

You did it! You have finished Volume I of Growing Up in Christ!!

Let me first say, "Thank you," for taking the time to read my book. I pray it blessed your spirit. It truly blessed me to write it, so know that you are greatly appreciated. I ask that you share this book with others.

As a reward and promised in the first chapter, here is an opportunity for you, if you choose to take me up on it. Go back to your notes at the end of each chapter. Read over them and make any necessary changes as the Lord lays it on your heart. Now transfer those notes collectively into the word processing program of your choice. Once transferred to a new document, you will have created your own version of 'Growing Up In Christ.'

That's right, I will be putting together an anthology for others to have the opportunity to share. This means, you like me and others, can become an author if you are so moved by the Lord. So, pray on it, fast and reach out should you choose to become a part of this 'growing' movement. You are more than welcome to simply share your story anonymously to help others 'Growing up in Christ,' without sharing your name. For more details and information, you can contact me by email: authormelspears@gmail.com. I look forward to hearing from you soon.

May the peace of the Lord fall on you and your household in Jesus Mighty name, Amen!

ABOUT THE AUTHOR

MEL SPEARS

Mel Spears is a faith-driven visionary, intercessor, and transformational leader called to restore hope, dignity, and spiritual alignment in the lives of women and families. She is the Founder and CEO of God's Women of Prayer, Power & Purpose, Inc., a 501(c)(3) nonprofit organization dedicated to equipping women and youth to rebuild their lives through discipleship, education, community care, and faith-based accountability.

With a heart for the broken, overlooked, and misunderstood, Mel combines prayer with practical strategy, offering not a handout, but a hand up, leading others into purpose through healing, obedience, and identity in Christ. Her mission is rooted in the belief that transformation begins the moment a person encounters both truth and love, and chooses to rise.

A powerful storyteller, Mel writes from a place of transparency and lived experiences. Her devotionals and teachings speak to the those who have survived disappointment, delay, spiritual warfare, and emotional heaviness, but refuses to die in the valley. Her voice is both prophetic and pastoral, guiding others through the process of inner restoration so they can walk in boldness, authority, and spiritual maturity.

Mel is a wife, a mother, mentor, and kingdom builder whose life testifies that healing is not the absence of pain, but the birth of purpose through it. She continues to serve communities across her hometown and beyond through outreach, leadership development, youth empowerment, and spiritual covering for those God has entrusted to her path.

She is not just building a movement, she is building legacies of faith, resilience, and kingdom impact.

www.ingramcontent.com/pod-product-compliance
Lightning Source LLC
Chambersburg PA
CBHW051241050726
47594CB00001B/263